AF790686

# KakaoTalk and Facebook

mediated youth

Sharon R. Mazzarella
*General Editor*

Vol. 33

The Mediated Youth series is part of the Peter Lang Media and Communication list.
Every volume is peer reviewed and meets
the highest quality standards for content and production.

PETER LANG
New York • Bern • Berlin
Brussels • Vienna • Oxford • Warsaw

Jiwoo Park & Dafna Lemish

# KakaoTalk and Facebook

## Korean American Youth Constructing Hybrid Identities

PETER LANG
New York • Bern • Berlin
Brussels • Vienna • Oxford • Warsaw

**Library of Congress Cataloging-in-Publication Data**

Names: Park, Jiwoo, author. | Lemish, Dafna, author.
Title: KakaoTalk and Facebook: Korean American youth constructing hybrid identities / Jiwoo Park and Dafna Lemish.
Description: New York: Peter Lang, 2019.
Series: Mediated youth; v. 33
ISSN 1555-1814 (print) | ISSN 2378-2935 (online)
Includes bibliographical references and index.
Identifiers: LCCN 2019006100 | ISBN 978-1-4331-5728-8 (hardback: alk. paper)
ISBN 978-1-4331-5729-5 (ebook pdf) | ISBN 978-1-4331-5730-1 (epub)
ISBN 978-1-4331-5731-8 (mobi)
Subjects: LCSH: Korean American youth—Ethnic identity.
Korean American youth—Social life and customs.
Korean Americans—Cultural assimilation.
Children of immigrants—Cultural assimilation.
Text messaging (Cell phone systems)—Social aspects. | Digital media—Social aspects.
Online social networks. | Transnationalism.
Classification: LCC E184.K6 P364 2019 | DDC 973/.04957—dc23
LC record available at https://lccn.loc.gov/2019006100
DOI 10.3726/b15438

Bibliographic information published by **Die Deutsche Nationalbibliothek**.
**Die Deutsche Nationalbibliothek** lists this publication in the “Deutsche Nationalbibliografie”; detailed bibliographic data are available on the Internet at http://dnb.d-nb.de/.

© 2019 Peter Lang Publishing, Inc., New York
29 Broadway, 18th floor, New York, NY 10006
www.peterlang.com

All rights reserved.
Reprint or reproduction, even partially, in all forms such as microfilm, xerography, microfiche, microcard, and offset strictly prohibited.

# CONTENTS

# FIGURES

# TABLES

# FOREWORD

This is a study on the lived experience of coming of age with a hybrid ethnic identity in the U.S. While we focus on the case study of Korean American youths, we believe it is exemplary of the larger phenomenon of immigration in the age of digital technology. While immigration just 100 years ago meant probably never seeing your family and friends again, and 50 years ago meant holding a rare and expensive phone call, today immigration entails daily video-chatting and the real-time exchanging of messages and photos as a taken-for-granted routine.

We approached this study as immigrants ourselves. While born and brought up in Seoul, Korea, Jiwoo studied as an international student in the U.S., away from the familiarity of home, in her early 20s. Dafna moved to the U.S. from Israel in her 50s, already an established scholar. We met at Southern Illinois University in Carbondale, Illinois, where Jiwoo was a Ph.D. student and Dafna was the Dean of the College of Mass Communication and Media Arts.

Our goal was to conduct this study with great compassion and empathy, since we both know from first-hand experience that digital technology is our lifeline to our roots, our families, our social networks, our mother tongue, and our homeland—all of which carry great emotional weight. When Jiwoo first moved to the U.S., she faced isolation from her family and friends, a language barrier, and stereotyping/discrimination. She struggled greatly to find her true identity as an international student, an identity which only stands out more when in conflict with mainstream American culture. Today, aided by KakaoTalk social networking application on her smartphone, with which she stays culturally informed and can communicate with the touch of a button with her family and friends in her homeland, she possesses a natural bent for blending two diverse cultures. This new reality has had a unique impact on her character and perspective. When Dafna was a graduate student in the U.S. in the late 1970s and early 1980s, she relied on weekly letters to stay connected with her family and the rare phone call to celebrate major life occasions, such as the birth of her first child. Today, she is constantly exchanging daily experiences in real time on WhatsApp with her family and close friends, and she keeps open internet links to Israeli news and cultural happenings, such as a newly published Hebrew book and a new vegan restaurant that opened in a remote village, which she plans to visit next time she travels back to Israel.

Our stories, however, are not unique. As a matter of fact, they are quite typical of the global immigration experience. Coming from these personal standpoints, though, we believe we were able to explore this particular case study of young Korean Americans with great care and nuance. Our journey was aided by many people. Jiwoo would first like to thank her family. She cannot express how grateful she is to her father, mother, older sister, and younger brother for all of the sacrifices that they have made on her behalf. Her special thanks go to Mark, her colleague and confidant, who offered his expert editorial input on her manuscript. She owes the most to Daniel Lee, her beloved other half, who recognized her academic potential and instilled in her a desire to explore with an inquisitive nature the identity construction process of the children of Korean immigrants in the U.S., a situation not unlike her own background. His clear and sharp intelligence, unconditional love, and prayers were what sustained her throughout this academic marathon. Dafna is grateful to her husband Peter and their children—Leeshai, Noam, Erga, and daughter-in-law Sarah—who have gone through the never-ending process of immigration themselves at different stages of their lives and have enriched her understanding of her own construction of an Israeli American identity in countless ways. We both wish to thank Dr. Sharon Mazzarella, the editor of the Mediated Youth series at Peter Lang, for believing in this book project from the start and for guiding us through the publishing process with support and invaluable editorial advice. We are also indebted to the Peter Lang's editorial and production team for their professionalism and dedication.

Last, but not least, we are enormously grateful to the many Korean American youths who shared their experiences with us and helped us understand their inner world. This book is for them and for our readers—we hope it will serve to help everyone understand and value the interconnections between technology and identity as well as themselves, whether they are immigrants or not.

# INTRODUCTION

> It was late in the afternoon, and Yoo Jin and Mi Young, two Korean American female teenagers, were chatting away in the food court at the mall, digging into a big bowl of *potbingsoo* (a traditional Korean dessert) while looking at their smartphones. Chan Soo, a Korean American male teenager, joined in, taking a sip of his soda as he sat down. He noted their smartphones on the table and said in Korean: "Who are you chatting with?" Yoo Jin answered, "We're having a group conversation about B.T.S." [an extremely popular South Korean K-pop boy band that won the Top Social Artist award at the 2017 and 2018 Billboard Music Awards] Chan Soo replied, "Yeah, and did you see their speech at the U.N. on YouTube? They made history—the first ever K-pop band to speak at the U.N.! Everyone online was talking about them and what they said" Mi Young commented, "Me, too, I am blown away by them. They made me so proud!"

While writing this book manuscript, the first author overheard this conversation while sitting next to the group of Korean American teenagers in the local food court at the mall. As this example indicates, one of the distinguishing features among Korean American youths in the digital age is their widespread use of smartphone-based KakaoTalk (a Korean mobile instant messaging application) communication and the powerful connectivity it fosters. With their smartphones in hand, they frequently check for KakaoTalk messages and share updates about K-pop stars, interactions that allow them to explore and commit to their ethnic identities in a way that reflects their relationship with their home country.

This book explores the role of digital media and the issue of ethnic identity through the eyes of a fast-expanding ethnic group: the children of Korean immigrants in the U.S. The year 2003 marked the centennial anniversary of Korean immigration to the U.S., but the majority of studies on Korean immigration have only focused on ethnic media, including satellite television, newspapers, and magazines (Lee, 2004; Moon & Park, 2007). Those studies also extensively examined media usage patterns and the role of traditional mass media in the process of integration as it applies to Korean adults, thereby excluding the children of Korean immigrants. Among the few studies that have dealt with the effect of media on the integration of Korean immigrants' children (Park, 2009), there is a near total absence of attention paid to present-day intersections of digital media and ethnic identity formation among these children. Therefore, examining how digital media enable the children of Korean immigrants to observe and investigate their ethnic identity formation as residents of the U.S. and assessing the degree of their assimilation into American society are a significant and necessary topic of study for its important implications for citizenship and culture.

In the contemporary globalized world, millions of people change their country of residence and live the life of a stranger in a foreign land. When immigrants migrate from their country of origin to one with an unfamiliar culture—in this case the American one—their children are caught between two worlds: the culture of their home country and their permanent locus in the American social environment. Among the long list of issues affecting the lives of immigrant descendants in the U.S. is how children formulate their ethnic identities while adapting to a new society, which becomes one of the most critical challenges in their lives. In the process of such geographical relocations, immigrant children neither absolutely resist their host country culture, nor do they entirely give up their original culture (Brinkerhoff, 2009). As Alba and Nee (1997) noted, immigrants' successful integration into a new society conventionally involves back-and-forth struggles between increasing exploration with one's new culture and still preserving one's original cultural connection. As it turns out, numerous prior studies suggest that immigrant children who maintain strong ties to their original culture and ethnicity tend to have healthier self-images and display more positive psychological well-being than those who are unable or choose not to do so (Phinney, 1990; Qin, 2006; Wakefield & Hudley, 2007).

One's ethnic identity formation process reflects various movements through complex social boundaries in global cultural systems (Giddens, 1984). However, those multi-cultural practices by diverse individuals do not follow a predetermined course, but are instead dependent upon media and communication technology available at any given time. Regarding the effects of digital media on the lives of immigrant children, online spaces have become a unique new public sphere that transcends the traditional perception of identity and brings numerous opportunities for youths with migrant backgrounds to explore their ethnic identities (Tan, 2005). In this era of continuous innovations in digital media technology, then, the descendants of immigrants have at their disposal ever more unique ways to vigorously engage with the intersection of their diverse cultural influences and ethnic backgrounds (Wong & Satzewich, 2006, p. 8).

As young immigrants are increasingly aware of diverse cultural information available online, the influence of digital media on their ethnic identity construction is of paramount concern to intercultural communication scholars (Chiang, 2010; Collier, 2000; Halualani, 2008; Koc, 2006). Furthermore, because digital media technology provides immigrant youth from every corner of the world with new methods of uniquely representing themselves and staying connected in online spaces, their ethnic identities that used to be location-specific and dependent on specific experiences native to those locations, are now subject to a process of constant transformation (Fitzgerald, 1992; Xie, 2005). Thus, with reference to the changing character of ethnic identities, it is worth exploring how immigrant children positioned between two cultures routinely (re)negotiate their ethnic identities in a world where an individual's self-perception is influenced by the diffusion of digital media devices.

In this study, we thus ask: What is the nature of the digital media practices of children of Korean immigrants in the U.S. in their socialization and in the development of their ethnic identity? How do they engage in the exploration of and commitment to their ethnic identity using the digital media devices at their disposal? How does digital media consumption affect this young population's assimilation into mainstream American society? In exploring these questions, we seek to contribute to the existing body of literature by elucidating how children of Korean immigrants in the U.S. are creatively using digital media technology to preserve and redefine their ethnic identity in the face of local assimilative forces.

## Book Outline

Chapter One of the book provides an overview of the theoretical grounding of the scholarship on immigration and assimilation in the U.S. and processes of identity formation. It also reviews the existing literature on the role of digital media practices in the digital diaspora. Chapter Two then focuses on the target group of Korean American youths and their experiences of being Korean American while providing information on the study's goals and methods.

Chapters Three, Four, and Five present the findings of the three main research questions, respectively. Chapter Three outlines the everyday digital practices of Korean American youths as compared to other American youths. Chapter Four explores more specifically the role of digital media in the construction of the Korean identity of these youths. These two chapters lead to the analyses offered in Chapter Five of the ways in which Korean American youths navigate their dual identities.

Chapter Six delves specifically into the related area of digital media bilingualism, which is central to identity formation. Finally, we conclude the book with an integrated discussion of the contribution of this study to our understanding of assimilation theories as well as to the central role digital media play in current processes of immigration. We also offer as Appendices more information about the two main tools of this study, for readers interested in the methodology.

## References

Alba, R., & Nee, V. (1997). Rethinking assimilation theory for a new era of immigration. *International Migration Review, 31*(4), 826–874.

Brinkerhoff, J. M. (2009). *Digital diasporas: Identity and transnational engagement*. Cambridge, UK: Cambridge University Press.

Chiang, C. Y. (2010). Diasporic theorizing paradigm on cultural identity. *Intercultural Communication Studies, 19*(1), 29–46.

Collier, M. J. (2000). Reconstructing cultural diversity in global relationships: Negotiating the borderlands. In G. M. Chen & W. J. Starosta (Eds.), *Communication and global society* (pp. 215–236). New York, NY: Peter Lang.

Fitzgerald, T. K. (1992). Media, ethnicity, and identity. In P. Scannell, P. Schlesinger, & C. Sparks (Eds.), *Culture and power* (pp. 112–133). London: Sage Publications.

Giddens, A. (1984). *The constitution of society*. Berkeley, CA: University of California Press.

Halualani, R. T. (2008). Where exactly is the Pacific? Global migration, diasporic movements, and intercultural communication. *Journal of International and Intercultural Communication, 1*, 3–22.

Koc, M. (2006). Cultural identity crisis in the age of globalization and technology. *The Turkish Online Journal of Educational Technology, 5*(1), 37–43.

Lee, C. (2004). Korean immigrants' viewing patterns of Korean satellite television and its role in their lives. *Asian Journal of Communication, 14*(1), 68–80.

Moon, S., & Park, C. (2007). Media effects on acculturation and biculturalism: A case study of Korean immigrants in Los Angeles' Koreatown. *Mass Communication & Society, 10*(3), 319–343.

Park, S. (2009). Negotiating identities and re-acculturation of second-generation Korean Americans: The role of ethnic media and peer group dynamics. *Korea Journal, 49*, 61–97.

Phinney, J. (1990). Ethnic identity in adolescents and adults: Review of research. *Psychological Bulletin, 108*(3), 499–514.

Qin, D. B. (2006). Our child doesn't talk to us anymore: Alienation in immigrant Chinese families. *Anthropology and Education Quarterly, 37*(2), 162–179.

Tan, S.-H. (Ed.). (2005). *Challenging citizenship: Group membership and cultural identity in a global age*. Burlington, VT: Ashgate.

Wakefield, W. D., & Hudley, C. (2007). Ethnic and racial identity and adolescent well-being. *Theories into Practice, 46*(2), 147–154.

Wong, L. L., & Satzewich, V. (2006). Introduction: The meaning and significance of transnationalism. In V. Satzewich & L. L. Wong (Eds.), *Transnational identities and practices in Canada* (pp. 1–17). Vancouver: UBC Press.

Xie, W. (2005). Virtual space, real identity: Exploring cultural identity of Chinese diaspora in virtual community. *Telematics and Informatics, 22*, 395–404.

· 1 ·

# IMMIGRATION AND IDENTITY FORMATION

## Immigration and Assimilation in the U.S.

Over the last few decades, new waves of immigration from all over the world have profoundly changed demographic realities in the U.S. and raised questions about assimilation into its culture. United States Census Bureau (2015) documented that 24% of all parents in the U.S. were immigrants, of them 32% originated in Latin America, 30% in Mexico, 23% in Asia, 8% in Europe, and 5% in Africa. Most prominently, new "second-generation" children of immigrants born in the U.S. or brought into the country at an early age have emerged as a significant and visible group. According to Portes and Rumbaut (2006), the number of children of immigrants in the U.S. surpassed 30 million in 2005. By 2050, if today's growth rate continues, one third of all Americans will be either Asian or Latinx. America today is thus very different from its previous iteration that welcomed European immigrants at the beginning of the twentieth century as it now reflects large-scale immigration of non-Europeans.

Given recent demographic trends, assimilation will clearly not apply to all immigrant minorities to the same extent, and this is one way in which the immigration stories of past and present are likely to differ. What might assimilation look like in the very complex landscape of twenty-first century immigration? In the political turmoil the country is facing as these lines are being written, it is unclear whether today's more open, inclusive America, where new immigrants from diverse backgrounds have more options to choose the pace and extent of their assimilation and decide their identities for themselves, will remain so in the future. Either way, reviewing the literature on Asian American assimilation presents a convincing picture that Asian American assimilation differs from that of European American or Latinx American, thereby evincing a different process of ethnic identity formation.

In the midst of this relatively new and very different wave of immigration, one particular debate that has drawn considerably wide scholarly attention is whether the longer recent immigrants and their descendants reside in the U.S., the more assimilated they will become. Essentially, when immigrants become assimilated, they often adopt the cultural ways of their host society and behave based on the norms and belief systems that characterize the dominant group. At the same time, they gain access to social and economic circles of mainstream society and learn to identify as Americans. However, despite the Americanization that today's immigrants already undergo, prior research found that some descendants of immigrants show a different pattern in which they, at younger ages, consider themselves American but increasingly adopt the ethnic identity of their parents as they grow older (Min, 2002; Min & Kim, 2000; Thai, 2002). Although U.S.-born children of immigrants are more likely to define themselves as Americans, there are several key factors that exert a turn away from American-made labels. For instance, these children often strive to fit into the mainstream and be included by the majority, but, simultaneously, family, peers, and the ethnic community may also heavily influence and affect their assimilation process. As a result, the children of immigrants have a double burden: attempting to fold both their original ethnic assets and new cultural elements into their individual identities and assimilating into the host society (Phinney, Romero, Nava, & Huang, 2001; Phinney & Rosenthal, 1992; Rumbaut, 1994).

Two main theoretical approaches in immigration literature have specifically attempted to explain assimilation phenomena of contemporary immigrants and their offspring: straight-line, or classical, assimilation and segmented assimilation theories (Portes & Zhou, 1993; Rumbaut, 1994). Since ethnic identity formation is inevitably connected to the process of assimilation, and in order to understand their overall adaptation to American society, it is important to distinguish and discuss these two assimilation theories and their components.

## Classical Assimilation Theory

According to earlier concepts of assimilation, over time, all immigrants and their descendants will give up their original cultural elements such as norms, beliefs, and traditions in favor of those of the mainstream host society. Based on this classical assimilation view proposed by Park and Burgess (1924), greater acceptance of the new culture and greater social relations with dominant members of the host society will lead to the gradual replacement of an immigrant's ethnic culture and co-ethnic networks with those of the host society. In other words, at the end of the process, the fading and final extinction of both ethnic identities and the cultural/social differences that mark immigrants in the U.S. is the result of complete assimilation (Alba & Nee, 1997; Gordon, 1964; Park, 1928; Warner & Srole, 1945).

Within this classical assimilation approach, a useful analysis is that of Gordon (1964), who developed a conceptual framework that better elucidated assimilation. Based upon his analysis, "seven dimensions—cultural, structural, identity, marital, prejudice, discrimination, and civic—provided a multidimensional index of assimilation that was used as an indicator in determining the degree of both individual and group assimilation" (Gordon, 1964, p. 34). Among these seven dimensions, he notably distinguished cultural assimilation from structural assimilation. The former refers to the degree to which immigrants and minority members adopt the cultural patterns of the host society, while the latter refers to immigrants' infinite access to formal social networks of the host society and high involvement in major associations and institutions of the dominant group (Hurh, 1998; Min & Kim, 2000). Gordon (1964) made the key argument that although ethnic minority groups could achieve cultural assimilation by their own efforts, their structural assimilation might not be as easily achievable despite their best efforts because it is controlled by the core group. Simply put, cultural assimilation occurs when immigrants and their children learn the American way of life; structural assimilation is likely to take place only under certain conditions in which immigrants and their offspring are socially allowed to join by members of the host society, especially by the core Anglo-Americans. As past studies reveal, despite a considerable degree of cultural assimilation of non-white minorities in the U.S., cultural assimilation is still not the sole condition for structural assimilation for many minorities in the U.S.

Another crucial aspect of a multidimensional concept of assimilation is identificational assimilation (Gans, 1979; Gordon, 1964), which is defined as the "development of [a] sense of peoplehood based exclusively on [the] host society" (Gordon, 1964, p. 71). As part of an individual's self-identity process, ethnic self-identification is defined as the "sense of oneself as a member of an ethnic group, possessing attributes common to that group" (Aboud, 1987, p. 32). For example, second generation descendants of immigrants may identify themselves as Americans, while first-and-a-half generation descendants of immigrants (i.e., those who were born and spent formative years in their home country before immigrating still as children) may identify with their parents' ethnic origins. This is an important issue to understand not only because it demonstrates a central aspect of assimilation, but also because previous research has documented that ethnic identity plays a significant role in other outcomes, such as immigrant children's academic achievement and psychological well-being (Arellano & Padilla, 1996; Rumbaut, 1994; Umaña-Taylor, 2004).

Traditional views of identificational assimilation have paid close attention to the experiences of the descendants of European immigrants (Alba, 1990; Bakalian, 1993; Gans, 1979). According to Gordon (1964), immigrants gradually cease defining themselves according to their ethnic identities and instead adopt a hyphenated-American identity (e.g., Irish-American, German-American, Norwegian-American) before formulating a sense of identity that is based exclusively on the host society. In other words, the final act of assimilation signifies giving up the hyphen in favor of a purely American identity (Golash-Boza, 2006). Based on the adaptation patterns of early European immigrants, this concept is regarded as part of the linear process of assimilation, which characterizes the gradual vanishing and eventual loss of ethnic identities in the U.S. (Portes & Rumbaut, 2001). Consequently, identificational assimilation is considered a one-way process in which immigrants will stop identifying with their ethnic origin and will ultimately choose American identities (Gordon, 1964). Essentially, these researchers believed that cultural, structural, and other kinds of assimilation would go on uninterrupted, without even slowing down, over several generations. Moreover, they thought that this assimilation process is nearly the same for all immigrants, even going so far as to illustrate the process on "a graph as a straight line: it began with the immigrants' arrival and ended when they had become fully American" (Gans, 2004, p. 37).

Although most prior research on immigration found advanced social and economic mobility among white European immigrants in the past, classical straight-line assimilation theory has come under fire for neglecting to distinguish between the assimilation processes of non-white ethnic groups and white ethnic groups (Alba & Nee, 1997; Portes, 1995; Portes & Zhou, 1993). For instance, previous research provides evidence of dissimilar consequences across individual members and ethnic groups, as well as a noticeable decrease in the overall well-being of descendants of non-white immigrants (Gans, 1992; Zhou, 1997). As Omi and Winant (1994) argue, ethnicity theory generally assumes rather than proves the similarity between non-white and white immigrant experiences through the use of the immigrant analogy. This blindspot of classical assimilation theory neglected the value and sustainability of ethnic minority cultures and also concealed barely-hidden ethnocentric assumptions about the superiority of Anglo-American culture (Alba & Nee, 2003). Another fatal problem in the traditional assimilation theory is that it does not allow any room for a positive role for the ethnic group and their cultural assets to play in the adaptation process. What early assimilationist scholars seemed to overlook was that, in some cases, when immigrant children are caught between two cultures and are unsure of which direction of assimilation is more desirable, family or ethnic community resources can play a positive role in counteracting an overriding inclination toward a negative form of acculturation that would result in the loss of his or her culture of origin.

## Segmented Assimilation Theory

In order to accommodate these emerging changes, a newer theoretical concept has been proposed called segmented assimilation, which supposes that there may be different paths of adaptation into the host society (Portes, 1995; Portes & Zhou, 1993; Zhou, 1997). According to segmented assimilation theory, assimilation is still occurring today as it did in the past for previous generations of immigrants; however, the important question is for what sector of contemporary society in the U.S. and in what social contexts does this divergent assimilation take place? Researchers on segmented assimilation theory recognize that the segments of society in which today's immigrants live display unique characteristics because of immigrants' different socioeconomic contexts, their culturally diverse backgrounds, and their non-white ethnic origins, and they understand how those different factors can affect the process of assimilation (Portes & Zhou, 1993).

Three processes of acculturation explain the correlations between immigrant children, their parents, and their ethnic community: consonant, dissonant, and selective. While immigrant parents and their children experience consonant acculturation by slowly forsaking their original culture and language and adopting those of the American mainstream at approximately the same speed, dissonant acculturation occurs when the descendants of immigrants acquire English and accept American ways more quickly than do their immigrant parents (Rumbaut, 1997, 2000). According to Portes and Rumbaut (2001), dissonant acculturation causes frequent conflicts between immigrant parents and their children and a disparity in communication between the generations. While children experiencing consonant acculturation are able to achieve upward mobility with the help of their parents, in the scenario of dissonant acculturation, they may tend toward downward mobility. Hence, there may be a close connection between parents' and children's acculturation because it affects the opportunities for immigrant children to take advantage of family and community resources when they are caught in a series of negative life events, including discrimination, while adjusting to the host society (Rumbaut & Portes, 2001).

In contrast to consonant and dissonant acculturation, selective acculturation takes place when both immigrant parents and their children gradually absorb American ways while still staying connected to their ethnic community in some aspects. It is described as retention of one's ethnic language along with English; therefore, immigrants speak their ethnic language at home whereas English is used in public life such as at school or work (Rumbaut, 1997, 2000). Coleman (1988) further argues that they develop more intimate family dynamics as cultural values, norms, and traditions can now be transmitted inter-generationally because immigrant children's fluency in their ethnic language allows them to maintain communication with their parents. Since transmission of language is inevitably tied to ethnic identity formation (Phinney, 1990, 1991), fluent bilingualism allows these children to resist identificational assimilation expected by the classical assimilation model to some degree, thereby helping them maintain a more ethnic identity (Sears, Fu, Henry, & Bui, 2003). In terms of a transformation in ethnic self-identification, it is apparent that those who are able to speak their ethnic language at home are more likely to maintain stable ethnic identities over time (Portes & Rumbaut, 2001). Furthermore, Portes and Rumbaut (2001) argue that the data show that fluently bilingual children not only have higher self-esteem and confidence, but generally do better academically.

As discussed above, based on the segmented assimilation perspective, the role that parents and extended family play in the transmission of culture and language as well as in the formulation of immigrant children's ethnic identity has been overlooked by the classical assimilation model (Cauce et al., 1992; Saenz, Hwang, Aguirre, & Anderson, 1995; Waters, 1990). For example, in Thai's (2002) study of Vietnamese Americans, most participants considered their parents as the most reinforcing agents of socialization who aid them in exploring and redefining their ethnic identity. Also, family structure is another factor that may play a vital role in ethnic identity development. In the cases of many Hispanic and Vietnamese descendants that have more family members, the variety of family arrangements may contribute to their active participation in their parents' original culture and preservation of their ethnic identities (Caplan, Choy, & Whitmore, 1992; Waggoner, 1988; Zhou & Bankston, 1994). Moreover, the at-home presence of extended family members or co-ethnics may reinforce immigrant children's ethnic identity formation because it creates a cultural environment in which they are exposed to their cultural values and norms (Rumbaut, 1994). Therefore, conformity to cultural norms, beliefs, and traditions prescribed by the family determine whether these contemporary immigrant children adopt or reject an American identity (Zhou & Bankston, 1998).

As detailed above, based upon segmented assimilation theory, assimilation is just one alternative among several distinct routes that immigrants and their descendants can choose in the American mainstream, meaning there is more than one way of becoming American (Bankston & Zhou, 1997; Zhou, 1997). In terms of ethnic identification within segmented assimilation theory, research shows a wealth of evidence concerning contemporary Asian American groups in the U.S. that points to a rejection of a loss of distinctive ethnic identities (Song, 2003). For example, on one hand, some immigrant children may choose assimilation and define themselves by their American identity; on the other hand, others may embrace their parents' ethnic background and define themselves by their ethnic identity. In other cases, some children are liable to combine selected aspects of their parents' national origin and American culture into their own hybridized ethnic identity (Waters, 1999). Therefore, immigrants' different characteristics at the time of their immigration and the varied social or economic circumstances they face within the host society will contribute to how different segments assimilate to American ways in the U.S., including their ethnic identity choices.

## Identity Formation

There has been an emergence of theories to address ethnic identity formation. One distinction in particular has shaped the way we look at how ethnic minorities adapt or acculturate in the U.S.: the notion of a fixed versus a fluid identity. As discussed above, classical assimilation theorists argue that minority immigrant groups will inevitably shed their culture and replace it with that of the mainstream society. Thus, all groups will eventually become one group with one culture, and physical differences will be difficult to identify due to a mass "melting" of the people (Glazer & Moynihan, 1970; Gordon, 1983; Parsons, 1964). According to this melting pot theory, immigrants' different cultural elements and cultural backgrounds blend and fuse together into "a new, unitary culture," which carries with it a quintessential "Americanness" and results in a new and unique American identity (Alba & Nee, 2003, p. 282). As far as the early theorists were concerned, since early European/Anglo immigrants had assimilated and become "white," the same inevitable fate was assumed to hold true for all "Americans." Thus, the notion of a fixed identity was widely accepted largely because people of color were completely absent from the dominant race discourse.

However, upon a closer look at contemporary immigrant groups' experiences, this is far from the truth. For example, several prior studies documented that certain second generation Asian American children may exhibit a pattern in which they eventually choose their parents' original ethnic identity as their own ethnic identities over time after initially resisting their ethnic backgrounds (Min, 2002; Min & Kim, 2000; Thai, 2002). Since 1965, changes in U.S. immigration policy (Kammer, 2015) have suggested that alternative assimilation patterns may exist as new legislation brought with it large scale immigration from Asia, in particular, introducing a new racial element into assimilation expectations. Although native-born adolescents are more likely to maintain or adopt American identities over time, a number of factors encourage a move away from American-made labels. As a result, ethnic minorities have constructed a new set of ethnic options that helps them navigate the tenuous racial terrain in the U.S.

In order to understand actual negotiation and construction in ethnic self-identification among immigrant children over time, it is important to discuss social construction theory, which argues that ethnicity is constructed and re-constructed in the context of social adjustment to a new society; therefore, ethnic self-identity is more likely to change over time (Barth, 1969; Hein,

1994; Lal, 2001; Omi & Winant, 1994; Tuan, 1998). With regard to ethnicity, there are two distinct theoretical approaches. On the one hand, the primordial perspective argues that ethnicity, including ethnic self-identification, is inherent because of common physical characteristics, language, values, beliefs, traditions, and history that are connected with one's original culture (Geertz, 1963). From this point of view, ethnicity is predetermined at birth, unalterable throughout the course of one's life, and regarded as an extension of blood ties (van den Berghe, 1978). This perspective implies that minority ethnic children have no choice in terms of their ethnic self-identification over time since it is innate.

However, unlike the primordial perspective of ethnicity, which refers to ethnicity as pre-given and static, the social construction perspective describes ethnicity, including self-identification, as fluctuating, situational, multiple, and dynamic (Nagel, 1994; Waters, 1990). Because it does not consider ethnicity to be innate, it argues that ethnicity can instead be socially constructed, maintained, reconfigured, and reformulated (Barth, 1969; Hein, 1994; Lal, 2001; Patterson, 1975). Furthermore, several recent scholars suggest that ethnic identity formation is an ongoing process that entails social interactions with other humans and their physical and social surroundings (Omi & Winant, 1994; Portes & Rumbaut, 2001; Rodríguez, 2000; Rodríguez & Cordero-Guzmán, 1992; Tuan, 1998; Waters, 1999).

Increasingly, more and more scholars insist that all other identities are contextual and fluid; therefore, identities are formulated and reformulated more specifically among minority ethnic youth groups, depending on the situation (Mitchell, 1974; Nagel, 1994; Okamura, 1994). Compared to classical assimilationists, who perceive identity as rigid and permanent, social constructionists posit that individual members of ethnic groups have their own perspective on how they should behave in a given situation. When immigrant children identify themselves as American, assimilationists describe the immigrant experience of becoming American as the final stage. However, social constructionists consider not only the nature of the situation whereby collective action is constructed, but also the individual's point of view (Lal, 1993). In this regard, immigrant children's ethnic identity formation should be negotiated within a number of different social contexts, such as the family, their ethnic friends, local peers, and society more generally (Song, 2003). It is therefore important to examine a number of different factors in ethnic identity formation research in order to understand the determinants of changes in ethnic self-identification.

## Phinney's Model of Ethnic Identity Development

Ethnic identity refers to the particular characteristics of an individual's relationship with his or her ethnic group (Phinney & Ong, 2007), and it has been conceptualized using both Tajfel's (1981) social identity theory and Erikson's (1968) identity formation theory. According to Tajfel's social identity theory, identity emerges out of an individual's perception of being a member of a particular group as well as the emotional quality that comes with that membership. Alternatively, Erikson's identity formation theory argues that identity development occurs in the process of navigating personal conflicts while exploring and committing to specific goals and values. While the former foregrounds the affective components of identity and how they are related to outcomes, the latter instead emphasizes the process of identity exploration and development.

According to developmental psychologists, from Erikson's perspective, individuals tend to develop strong ethnic identities through the processes of exploring the meaning of and a sense of commitment to that identity (Phinney, 1996; Phinney & Ong, 2007; Quintana, 2007; Wakefield & Hudley, 2007). Exploration usually occurs at the outset of ethnic identity development (Phinney & Ong, 2007). Individuals engaged in exploration tend to investigate and learn more about the meaning of their ethnic background (Phinney & Ong, 2007; Wakefield & Hudley, 2007). Exploration can involve a range of activities, such as eating ethnic food, using a native language, interacting with members of one's ethnic group, reading books about one's ethnic heritage, learning cultural practices, and participating in cultural events. However, of great importance here is that exploration is a multidimensional construct, because individuals' methods of exploration—from listening to ethnic music to participating in cultural events—may differ greatly from one another. Similarly, individuals may actively attend certain events either to explicitly learn about their heritage or to affirm a sense of ethnic belonging, both of which also demonstrate varied levels of exploration and commitment.

Although exploration is most common in adolescence, it can occur at any point during an individual's lifetime and may possibly continue throughout one's entire life (Phinney, 2006), depending on individual experiences. Individuals who engage in identity exploration prior to commitment tend to have a firmer understanding of their ethnic identity because through the process of exploration, they better understand what that identity means and how best to express it (Phinney & Ong, 2007). Thus, exploration is important to the process of ethnic identity formation because without it, one's commitment may be too easily influenced by new experiences.

Commitment is one of the most crucial components of ethnic identity achievement (Phinney & Ong, 2007). Commitment refers to the process of fostering ties with and developing a sense of membership to one's particular ethnic group. Individuals engage in the process of commitment by developing and internalizing feelings of belonging with regards to their ethnic group (Phinney & Ong, 2007). More so than a sense of belonging or membership, it is also the process wherein an individual decides the extent to which he or she embraces and values ethnicity as part of his or her personal identity (Wakefield & Hudley, 2007). Therefore, individuals engaged in commitment are negotiating both how they perceive themselves in a group context as well as how comfortable they are foregrounding their group ties when they find themselves in a different context.

Commitment to the group associated with one's ethnic identity not only speaks to his or her process of identity negotiation, but it also gives him or her access to important human resources that may be unavailable to those who have not committed. Communities are sources of peers who can leverage their familiarity with the complexities of adolescence to convince youths to make mature and productive life choices (Evans-Winters, 2005). Peers can also help youths develop positive ethnicized self-concepts by recognizing bigotry and oppression from outsiders, sharing with each other ways to cope with and resist such oppression, and publicly showing pride in their shared culture (Evans-Winters, 2005; Teranishi, 2002; Tuan, 1998). Previous studies show that connections with community members of the same ethnic background play a significant role in positive psychological well-being because ethnic communities provide vital support systems for adolescent youth who are marginalized due to their ethnic identities (Arellano & Padilla, 1996; Rumbaut, 1994; Umaña-Taylor, 2004).

In terms of ethnic identity, Phinney (1989) drew on Tajfel's and Erikson's theories in designing the Multigroup Ethnic Identity Measure (MEIM) as a measure of one's perception of group membership. Its purpose was to broadly measure ethnic identity across three interrelated aspects: "ethnic identity achievement," "affirmation and belonging," and "ethnic behaviors." Phinney (1992) argued that these aspects play a crucial role in how ethnic minorities in the U.S. maintain self-esteem and develop a sense of belonging, particularly when they are confronted with prejudice and discrimination. Their ethnic identity formation therefore has broader implications with regard to society as a whole, with an unsuccessful resolution resulting in a lack of clarity about oneself and one's place in society and a successful resolution, or ethnic identity achievement, indicating a secure sense of self (Erikson, 1968).

Phinney's (1992) MEIM includes 14 items that comprehensively assess individuals' degree of identity exploration, level of commitment, participation in ethnic cultural activities, and affirmation and belonging regarding their ethnic group. Each item is rated on a 4-point scale from 1 (strongly disagree) to 4 (strongly agree). The resulting composite score of all of the items is then used to determine one's degree of ethnic identity achievement, with a higher score representing a more positive ethnic identity.

Recently, Phinney and Ong (2007) revised the MEIM by reducing the number of items and distributing them equally across two subscales—exploration and commitment—which allows both to be weighted equally in order to improve content and face validity. In the resulting Multigroup Ethnic Identity Measure–Revised (MEIM–R), the ethnic identity exploration and commitment subscales each consist of a distinct set of three items rated on a 5-point scale from 1 (strongly disagree) to 5 (strongly agree). Each item within each subscale is positively worded, and all of the items across both subscales are averaged together so that higher values represent greater ethnic identity achievement. For research purposes, however, the two subscales can also be used separately to gain greater insight into the differing implications of exploration and commitment (French, Seidman, Allen, & Aber, 2006). Thus, the MEIM–R provides a concise measure of the core aspects of group identity that determine the foundational strength of an individual's ethnic identity, or the degree to which his or her ethnic identity has been achieved (Syed & Azmitia, 2009; Yoon, 2011). The final list of the 6 items in the MEIM–R is shown in Appendix B.

In summary, both segmented assimilation theory and social construction theory are useful in seeking to understand how ethnic identity is negotiated and constructed among the children of Korean immigrants in the U.S., the former because it assumes multiple ways of becoming American (Bankston & Zhou, 1997; Zhou, 1997) and the latter because it posits that ethnic identity may be questioned, explored, and reformulated (Lal, 1993; Nagel, 1994). In addition, Phinney's model of ethnic identity development and the concepts of exploration and commitment are crucial to this study's analysis of how such children explore and commit to their ethnic identity while immersed in the influence of digital media technology. These three theories collectively represent the theoretical framework of the present study, which analyzes how the children of Korean immigrants in the U.S. use digital media devices to explore and commit to their ethnic identity even while dealing with the pressures of assimilation.

## The Digital Diaspora and Digital Media Practice

The term "diaspora," which is defined as "the segment of a people living outside the homeland" (Connor, 1986, p. 160), conveys different meanings and includes historical phenomena such as globalization, translocalities, and the crisis of the traditional state. Today, the term diaspora makes two main assumptions. The first assumption is that there was a single locale from which all people who identify as a particular ethnicity originated. The second assumption is that even as they live away from the original location, these communities maintain versions or remnants of customs and cultural practices as part of their ethnic identity. While people in diaspora may be integrated into their host society, their ties with their ancestral home often remain salient through the deployment of these customs and practices, or, as Gans (1979) calls it, "symbolic ethnicity" (p. 22).

In a high-technology society, the notion of diaspora has also evolved into that of a digital diaspora. According to Laguerre's (2010) definition, "a digital diaspora is an immigrant group or descendant of an immigrant population that use IT connectivity to participate in virtual networks of contacts for a variety of political, economic, social, religious, and communicational purposes that, for the most part, may concern either the homeland, and the host land, or both, including its own trajectory abroad" (p. 50). A digital diaspora navigates its international arena of practice in a universe dotted with the homeland and diverse host lands as the primary foci of its digital interventions (Laguerre, 2010, p. 63). This leads to a flexible regime of practice, which makes it possible for the activities in which diasporas engage to take different virtual forms. However, digital diasporas differ from virtual communities because digital diasporas have strong ties to real nations before they create or re-create the digital community (Alonso & Oiarzabal, 2010, p. 11).

The formation of ethnic identity usually takes place through the process of social interaction, which is conducted on the basis of social settings in certain physical boundaries, and the characteristics of ethnic identity construct the accepted notions of community (Chen & Dai, 2012, p. 125). However, this traditional meaning of individual or collective ethnic identity and community has been disrupted by innovations in information and communication technology (Kraidy, 2002; Tenenboim-Weinblatt, 2010). As people move through these multiple cultural spaces using digital media, it allows individuals to communicate more directly and more regularly with persons living in other cultures, synthesize diverse cultural elements, and even extend their identities. These mutual online exploring and learning processes help people to adopt a flexible viewpoint through which they can see themselves with new cultural eyes through other participants' responses. Thus, by changing the concept of territorially confined ethnic identity through digital media, people can potentially reinterpret their sense of identity and cultivate the future development of their ethnic identities on the basis of diverse experiences gained in the digital world (Chen & Dai, 2012, p. 127).

One additional critical component of this contemporary process of change is the potential facilitated by digital media for the construction of ethnic identities and global ties that express and represent non-Western values, norms, and lifestyles. These processes are taking place as a greater diversity of social and cultural participants around the world interact within and across cultures using a spectrum of digital media (Cheong, Martin, & Macfadyen, 2012). Various forms and functions of digital media have transformed the way the digital diaspora interact across different cultures and within different intra-cultural groups.

## Young Immigrants and Digital Media Practices

In the last two decades, digital media, especially social media such as Facebook, Twitter, and YouTube, have gained undeniable momentum. In light of their functional innovations, they help people, particularly immigrant children, overcome physical distances to communicate and engage with information easily, potentially initiating intercultural dialogues (Kaplan, 2010; Notafish, 2010). With the help of digital media, these immigrant children now have access to multiple models of ethnic identities, cultural lifestyles, and non-Western beliefs. The global connectedness of digital media due to time-space compression appears to provide an important platform for the development of friendships and relationships that are instrumental in ethnic identity formation among the younger generation of immigrants (boyd & Ellison, 2007; McPhail, 2006). Through virtual socialization, youth learn ways of exploring and obtaining their ethnic background and social status regarding their ethnic identities. Due to the creative ways they use this technology, these practices create numerous opportunities for them to form a cyber-community and formulate a new ethnic identity (Chen & Zhang, 2010).

According to Elias and Lemish (2009), one of the central roles the internet plays for immigrant youths is as a safe arena for experimenting with social interactions with local peers as well as social networking with their co-ethnics (p. 4). Shao (2009) similarly found that YouTube is used for social connections, information searching, and entertainment, as well as for self-actualization and the self-expression of one's ethnic identity. Young web users can now therefore choose among a variety of media to explore and construct their ethnic identities, such as e-mail, Twitter, chat rooms, blogs, and Social Networking Sites (SNSs) (boyd & Ellison, 2007; McPhail, 2006).

When individuals of diverse cultural backgrounds interact online, issues of culture, ethnicity, gender, and identity come into play (Yang, 2012). The specific sites that participants visit online significantly affect the stability and fluidity of their ethnic identities. In this sense, the growing use of digital media by ethnic minority groups in all corners of the world has profound communicative implications and consequences (Mehra, Merkel, & Bishop, 2004). Thus, the increasing incorporation of digital media into diaspora's everyday lives facilitates a de-territorialization that erodes the traditional relationship between culture and geographical/social territories and gives them a sense that they can start over from the beginning as an individual with re-defined ethnic identities through interactions in cyberspace (Garcia-Canclini, 1995; Tomlinson, 1999).

When positioned between two cultural worlds, such immigrant children have to further endure ongoing processes of "reformulating" their identities by moving between two environments (Bourdieu, 1990, 1998). This oscillation between assimilation and resistance is central to the formation of ethnic identity. Considering media exposure as one of the factors that influence one's degree of cultural adaptation to the host country (Gibson, 2001; Hovey, 2000), digital media play a substantial role among digital diasporas. In particular, they facilitate young descendants' back-and-forth movement between the two cultures of which they are a part—what is referred to as "keeping feet in both worlds" (Levitt, 2003, p. 177). Yi's (2009) discussion of the online activities of a local community of Korean American teenagers in the Midwestern U.S. is a supporting example of this phenomenon. As shown in her analysis, a plentiful blending of Korean and English and customary references to practices in both Korea and the U.S. were revealed in their instant messaging (IM) screen names and website postings to one another. The websites using both Korean and English have a vitally instrumental role in helping these second generation Korean Americans build "a newly emerging hybrid cultural realm," as in the case of Former Soviet Union adolescents in Israel (Elias & Lemish, 2008, p. 173), that captures both aspects of Korean and American cultures by providing a bi-cultural space that mixes Korean and American lifestyles.

Another example is Han's (2012) research of the online socialization of a local community church of Korean Australian teenagers in Melbourne, Australia. In his study, these young immigrants used the bulletin board on the church website as a bi-cultural space that reflects both Korean and Australian issues. One of the common interests they shared was sports, as witnessed in their strong support for Korean national teams and expressions of long-distance nationalism (Waldinger & Fitzgerald, 2004). The Red Devils' (the name of the cheering group) cheering for Korea's national soccer team during every World Cup is an example of how Korean diaspora utilizes the media in some respects more like Koreans (Lowe-Lee, 2010). According to another posting on the World Cup, a group of young members wearing "Be the Reds!" t-shirts gathered in a member's home to watch and cheer for the Korean national soccer team using satellite television. After watching the World Cup together, they frequently visited the bulletin board and shared how this occasion promoted a sense of pride for the Korean Australian community. The Red Devil Fever that has fueled nationalistic sentiments in contemporary Korean Australians is an important turning point that has allowed Korean Australian children to be proud of having Korean cultural heritage. In this context, the church website bulletin board became an effective communication channel for exchanging personal experiences that are associated with "Koreanness" in the host society.

Scholars have also noticed the significance of a particular computer-mediated communication (CMC) context when studying identity formation and expression in online encounters (Dervin & Abbas, 2009; Chester & Bretherton, 2007). One function of SNSs is associated with identity experimentation (Pearson, 2009). When casually checking a friend's page on an SNS or updating a profile on Facebook, a participant unconsciously or consciously makes a series of decisions that reflect and facilitate the process of identification (Rybas, 2012, p. 95). In other words, their cultural selves are revealed by the way they speak and the behaviors they perform online. The unique context of cyberspace, as a space in which descendants of immigrants from different cultures coexist, gives participants more power in constructing and expressing identities on the internet, which makes their identities more evolving (Yang, 2012, p. 118). Therefore, immigrant children whose identities seem to be increasingly in a state of flux cultivate themselves in everyday life by oscillating between different cultural value systems using their SNSs.

Another aspect of the digital media environment of digital diaspora families is the use of communication technologies for maintaining family ties and social relationships across borders. IM has become increasingly known as a popular form of mediated communication, particularly among teenagers (Boneva, Quinn, Kraut, Kiesler, & Shklovski, 2006). Unlike asynchronous email exchanges, IM reinforces real-time, second-by-second, "instant" message exchanges between participants. In contemporary mobile-saturated society, youth constantly use smartphones for immediate communication with their family and peer group beyond time and space via internet sites such as Facebook. In a sense, smartphones transcend family fragmentation and allow one to keep kin or friends connected in intimate ways not previously available, because regardless of where they are and what they are doing, they can be reached individually (Cheong et al., 2012). For instance, Valkenburg and Peter's (2009) research, based on a longitudinal study of Dutch teenagers, revealed that these teenagers are involved with sharing highly personal agendas or matters using IM that they would not otherwise easily share in a face-to-face interaction. Because of the rapid diffusion of smartphones and the unique youth culture that has developed as a result (Ito et al., 2008), children can create their own private time/space in public. As can be readily observed, prevalent mobile technologies have given new opportunities for subjectivity, alternative ways of presenting emotions, struggles, gender, and sociality, as well as a performative space to negotiate identity (Kim, 2009).

The interactivity and hypertextuality of digital media provide users with resources within the interconnected nodes of the internet and a space to develop virtual experiences and realities (Chen & Dai, 2012, p. 124). Digital media forms, such as SNSs, handheld devices, and the "do-it-yourself" (DIY) culture born out of new information and communication technologies (Ng, 2012, p. 258), generate a creative atmosphere for these young children to project their self-image and construct new realities in the comfort of their chosen space and time (Kim, 2009). An example of this phenomenon, one that redefines the role of cultural consumers by enabling both media consumption and media production, is the way in which young people around the globe share their own self-representations in the virtual environment of YouTube (Thomas, 2011).

However, researchers are at odds over the authenticity of cultural expressions within virtual communities. More so than influencing media consumption and production, according to Gajjala (2004), cyberspace today looks white because people of different races, genders, ethnicities, and nationalities are all connected within "Westernized, Anglicized and white cyberspace" (p. 84). In contrast, Nakamura (2007), in her research of Asian American internet tactics, argues that "manifestations of expressive cultures on the internet may ... provide an online oasis or refuge for users of color" (p. 183). Also, she argues that "cyberspace functions as a vector for resistant cultural practices that allow Asian Americans to both use and produce cyberspace" (p. 185). However, the approach should not be how ethnic minorities may overcome obstacles to access so that they may join "mainstream" America as consumers of the internet, but how users of digital media technologies can creatively express more richly layered and varied ethnic identities, thereby helping the audience more fully embrace a different and more diverse portrait of America (Ng, 2012, p. 269).

In intercultural online communication, descendants of immigrants prefer to be recognized and accepted, but they also desire to be independent and differentiated so that both self- and mutual identification can be accomplished (Dougherty, Mobley, & Smith, 2010). When young minority individuals, clouded by their identification with the dominant culture, adopt the mainstream culture without differentiating themselves from cultural others, the consequence will be either assimilation or over-accommodation. According to Dai (2010) and Gallois, Ogay, and Giles (2005), neither assimilation nor over-accommodation will develop reciprocal relationships since the former makes these children feel that they are suppressed, whereas the latter makes them feel that they are treated as incompetent. As one way to resist against assimilation or over-accommodation, immigrant children's integration of digital media into everyday life may introduce to them diverse cultural experiences and provide new ways of exploring their ethnic culture and identity or representing their ethnic culture and identity at both local and global levels (Zou & Trueba, 1998). In a virtual environment, the negotiation and expression of ethnic identity are related to cultural norms as well as the specific contexts in which they take place (Yang, 2012). In this regard, the investigation of the negotiation and expression of ethnic identity requires an in-depth inquiry into complex online communication processes.

## References

Aboud, F. E. (1987). The development of ethnic self-identification and attitudes. In J. S. Phinney & M. J. Rotheram (Eds.), *Children's ethnic socialization: Pluralism and development* (pp. 32–55). Newbury Park, CA: Sage Publications.

Alba, R. D. (1990). *Ethnic identity: The transformation of white America*. New Haven, CT: Yale University Press.

Alba, R., & Nee, V. (1997). Rethinking assimilation theory for a new era of immigration. *International Migration Review, 31*(4), 826–874.

Alba, R., & Nee, V. (2003). *Remaking the American mainstream: Assimilation and contemporary immigration*. Cambridge, MA: Harvard University Press.

Alonso, A., & Oiarzabal, P. J. (2010). *Diaspora in the new media age: Identity, politics, and community*. Reno, NV: University of Nevada Press.

Arellano, A. R., & Padilla, A. M. (1996). Academic invulnerability among a select group of Latino university students. *Hispanic Journal of Behavioral Sciences, 18*(4), 485–507.

Bakalian, A. (1993). *Armenian-Americans: From being to feeling Armenian*. New Brunswick, NJ: Transaction.

Bankston III, C. L., & Zhou, M. (1997). The social adjustment of Vietnamese American adolescents: Evidence for a segmented-assimilation approach. *Social Science Quarterly, 78*(2), 508–523.

Barth, F. (1969). *Ethnic groups and boundaries*. Boston, MA: Little, Brown.

Boneva, B. S., Quinn, A., Kraut, R. E., Kiesler, S., & Shklovski, I. (2006). Teenage communication in the instant messaging era. In R. Kraut, M. Brynin, & S. Kiesler (Eds.), *Computers, phones, and the Internet: Domesticating information technology* (pp. 201–218). New York, NY: Oxford University Press.

Bourdieu, P. (1990). *The logic of practice* (R. Nice, Trans.). Cambridge, UK: Polity Press.

Bourdieu, P. (1998). *Practical reason: On the theory of action*. Cambridge, UK: Polity Press.

boyd, d. m., & Ellison, N. B. (2007). Social network sites: Definition, history, and scholarship. *Journal of Computer-Mediated Communication, 13*, 210–230.

Caplan, N., Choy, M. H., & Whitmore, J. K. (1992). *Children of the boat people: A study of educational success*. Ann Arbor MI: University of Michigan Press.

Cauce, A. M., Hiraga, Y., Mason, C., Aguilar, T., Ordonez, N., & Gonzales, N. (1992). Between a rock and a hard place: Social adjustment of biracial youth. In M. P. P. Root (Eds.), *Racially mixed people in America* (pp. 207–222). Newbury Park, CA: Sage Publications.

Chen, G. M., & Dai, X. (2012). New media and asymmetry in cultural identity negotiation. In P. H. Cheong, J. N. Martin, & L. P. Macfadyen (Eds.), *New media and intercultural communication: Identity, community, and politics* (pp. 123–133). New York, NY: Peter Lang.

Chen, G. M., & Zhang, K. (2010). New media and cultural identity in the global society. In R. Taiwo (Ed.), *Handbook of research on discourse behavior and digital communication: Language structures and social interaction* (pp. 801–815). Hershey, PA: Idea Group.

Cheong, P. H., Martin, J. N., & Macfadyen, L. P. (2012). *New media and intercultural communication: Identity, community, and politics*. New York, NY: Peter Lang.

Chester, A., & Bretherton, D. (2007). Impression management and identity online. In A. N. Joinson, K. Y. A. McKenna, T. Postmes, & U.-D. Reips (Eds.), *The Oxford handbook of Internet psychology* (pp. 223–236). New York, NY: Oxford University Press.

Coleman, J. S. (1988). Social capital in the creation of human capital. *American Journal of Sociology, 94*, 95–120.

Connor, W. (1986). The impact of homelands upon diasporas. In G. Sheffer (Ed.), *Modern diasporas in international politics* (pp. 16–46). New York, NY: St. Martin's.

Dai, X. D. (2010). Intersubjectivity and interculturality: A conceptual link. *China Media Research*, *6*(1), 12–19.

Dervin, F., & Abbas, Y. (2009). Introduction. In Y. Abbas & F. Dervin (Eds.), *Digital technologies of the self* (pp. 1–11). Newcastle, UK: Cambridge Scholars.

Dougherty, D. S., Mobley, S. K., & Smith, S. E. (2010). Language convergence and meaning divergence: A theory of intercultural communication. *Journal of International and Intercultural Communication*, *3*(2), 164–186.

Elias, N., & Lemish, D. (2008). The Internet life of Former Soviet Union adolescents in Israel. In I. Rydin & U. Sjöberg (Eds.), *Mediated crossroads: Identity, youth culture and ethnicity—Theoretical and methodological challenges* (pp. 173–192). Göteborg, Sweden: Nordicom, Göteborg University.

Elias, N., & Lemish, D. (2009). Spinning the web of identity: The roles of the internet in the lives of immigrant adolescents. *New Media & Society*, *11*(4), 1–19.

Erikson, E. (1968). *Identity: Youth and crisis*. New York, NY: W. W. Norton.

Evans-Winters, E. (2005). *Teaching black girls: Resiliency in urban classrooms*. New York, NY: Peter Lang.

French, S., Seidman, E., Allen, L., & Aber, J. L. (2006). The development of ethnic identity during adolescence. *Developmental Psychology*, *42*(1), 1–10.

Gajjala, R. (2004). Negotiating cyberspace/Negotiating RL. In A. Gonzalez, M. Houston, & V. Chen (Eds.), *Our voices* (pp. 82–91). Los Angeles, CA: Roxbury.

Gallois, C., Ogay, T., & Giles, H. (2005). Communication accommodation theory: A look back and a look ahead. In W. B. Gudykunst (Ed.), *Theorizing about intercultural communication* (pp. 121–148). Thousand Oaks, CA: Sage Publications.

Gans, H. J. (1979). Symbolic ethnicity: The future of ethnic groups and cultures in America. *Ethnic and Racial Studies*, *2*(1), 1–20.

Gans, H. J. (1992). Second-generation decline: Scenarios for the economic and ethnic futures of the post-1965 American immigrants. *Ethnic and Racial Studies*, *15*(2), 173–192.

Gans, H. J. (2004). The American kaleidoscope, then and now. In T. Jacoby (Ed.), *Reinventing the melting pot: The new immigrants and what it means to be American* (pp. 33–45). New York, NY: Basic Books.

Garcia-Canclini, N. (1995). *Hybrid cultures: Strategies for entering and leaving modernity*. Minneapolis, MN: University of Minnesota Press.

Geertz, C. (Ed.). (1963). The integrative revolution: Primordial sentiments and civil politics in the new states. In C. Geertz (Ed.), *Old societies and new states* (pp. 105–157). New York, NY: Free Press.

Gibson, M. (2001). Immigrant adaptation and patterns of acculturation. *Human Development*, *44*, 19–23.

Glazer, N., & Moynihan, D. P. (1970). *Beyond the melting pot: The Negroes, Puerto Ricans, Jews, Italians, and Irish of New York City*. Cambridge, MA: MIT Press.

Golash-Boza, T. (2006). Dropping the hyphen? Becoming Latino(a)-American through racialized assimilation. *Social Forces*, *85*(1), 27–55.

Gordon, M. (1964). *Assimilation in American life*. New York, NY: Oxford University Press.

Gordon, M. (1983). *America as a multicultural society*. Philadelphia, PA: American Academy of Political and Social Science.

Han, G. S. (2012). *Korean diaspora and media in Australia: In search of identities*. Lanham, MD: University Press of America.

Hein, J. (1994). From migrant to minority: Hmong refugees and the social construction of identity in the United States. *Sociological Inquiry*, *64*(3), 281–306.

Hovey, J. (2000). Acculturative stress, depression and suicidal ideation among Central American immigrants. *Suicide & Life-Threatening Behavior*, *30*(2), 125–139.

Hurh, W. M. (1998). *The Korean Americans*. Westport, CT: Greenwood Press.

Ito, M., Horst, H., Bittanti, M., boyd, d., Herr-Stephenson, B., & Lange, P. G, … Robinson, L. (2008). *Living and learning with new media: Summary of findings from the Digital Youth Project*. Chicago: The John D. and Catherine T. MacArthur Foundation.

Kammer, J. (2015). *The Hart-Celler Immigration Act of 1965: Political figures and historic circumstances produced dramatic, unintended consequences*. Retrieved from https://cis.org/sites/cis.org/files/kammer-hart-celler.pdf

Kaplan, A. M. (2010). Users of the world, unite! The challenges and opportunities of social media. *Business Horizons*, *53*(1), 59–68.

Kim, Y. (2009). *Media consumption and everyday life in Asia*. London: Routledge.

Kraidy, M. M. (2002). Hybridity in cultural globalization. *Communication Theory*, *12*(3), 316–339.

Laguerre, M. S. (2010). Digital diaspora: Definition and models. In A. Alonso & P. J. Oiarzabal (Eds.), *Diaspora in the new media age: Identity, politics, and community* (pp. 49–64). Reno: University of Nevada Press.

Lal, B. B. (1993). The celebration of ethnicity as a critique of American life: Opposition to Robert E. Park's view of cultural pluralism and democracy. In R. Gubert & L. Tomasi (Eds.), *Robert E. Park and the "Melting Pot"* Trento, Italy: Reverdito Edizioni.

Lal, B. B. (2001). Learning to do ethnic identity. In D. Parker & M. Song (Eds.), *Rethinking "mixed race"* (pp. 154–172). London: Pluto Press.

Levitt, P. (2003). Keeping feet in both worlds: Transnational practices and immigrant incorporation in the United States. In C. Joppke & E. Morawska (Eds.), *Toward assimilation and citizenship: Immigrants in liberal nation-states* (pp. 177–194). New York, NY: Palgrave Macmillian.

Lowe-Lee, F. (2010, May 12). Red Devils created global culture of street cheering. *The Korea Times*. Retrieved from http://www.koreatimes.co.kr/www/news/biz/2010/05/291_65771.html

McPhail, T. (2006). *Global communication: Theories, stakeholders and trends*. (2nd ed.). Malden, MA: Wiley-Blackwell.

Mehra, B., Merkel, C., & Bishop, A. P. (2004). The Internet for empowerment of minority and marginalized users. *New Media & Society*, *6*(6), 781–802.

Min, P. G. (2002). Introduction. In P. G. Min (Ed.), *The second generation: Ethnic identity among Asian Americans* (pp. 1–18). Walnut Creek, CA: AltaMira Press.

Min, P. G., & Kim, R. (2000). Formation of ethnic and racial identities: Narratives by young Asian-American professionals. *Ethnic and Racial Studies*, *23*(4), 735–760.

Mitchell, J. C. (1974). Perception of ethnicity and ethnic behavior: An empirical exploration. In A. Cohen (Ed.), *Urban ethnicity* (pp. 1–36). London: Tavistock.

Nagel, J. (1994). Constructing ethnicity: Creating and recreating ethnic identity and culture. *Social Problems*, *41*(1), 152–176.

Nakamura, L. (2007). *Digitizing race: Visual cultures of the Internet*. Minneapolis, MN: University of Minnesota Press.

Ng, K. (2012). Asian American new media communication as cultural engagement: E-mail, vlog/blogs, mobile applications, social networks, and YouTube. In P. H. Cheong, J. N. Martin, & L. P. Macfadyen (Eds.), *New media and intercultural communication: Identity, community, and politics* (pp. 79–106). New York, NY: Peter Lang.

Notafish. (2010, October 16). How intercultural is social media? [web log post]. Retrieved from http://blog.notanendive.org/post/2010/09/19/how-intercultural-is-social-media

Okamura, J. (1994). Why there are no Asian Americans in Hawaii: The continuing significance of local identity. *Social Process in Hawaii, 35*, 161–178.

Omi, M., & Winant, H. (1994). *Racial formation in the United States*. New York, NY: Routledge.

Park, R. E. (1928). Human migration and the marginal man. *American Journal of Sociology, 33*(6), 881–893.

Park, R. E., & Burgess, E. W. (1924). *Introduction to the science of sociology*. (2nd ed.). Chicago, IL: The University of Chicago Press.

Parsons, T. (1964). *Social structure and personality*. New York, NY: Free Press of Glencoe.

Patterson, O. (1975). Context and choice in ethnic allegiance. In N. Glazer & D. Moynihan (Eds.), *Ethnicity: Theory and experience* (305–349). Cambridge, MA: Harvard University Press.

Pearson, E. (2009). All the World Wide Web's a stage: The performance of identity in online social network sites. *First Monday*, *14*(3). Retrieved from http://firstmonday.org/ojs/index.php/fm/article/view/2162

Phinney, J. (1989). Stages of ethnic identity development in minority group adolescents. *Journal of Early Adolescence*, 9, 34– 49.

Phinney, J. (1990). Ethnic identity in adolescents and adults: Review of research. *Psychological Bulletin*, *108*(3), 499–514.

Phinney, J. (1991). Ethnic identity and self-esteem: A review and integration. *Hispanic Journal of Behavioral Sciences*, *13*(2), 193–208.

Phinney, J. (1992). The multigroup ethnic identity measure: A new scale for use with diverse groups. *Journal of Adolescent Research*, *7*(2), 156–176.

Phinney, J. (1996). Understanding ethnic diversity: The role of ethnic identity. *American Behavior Scientist*, *40*(2), 143–152.

Phinney, J. (2006). Ethnic identity exploration in emerging adulthood. In J. Arnett & J. L. Tanner (Eds.), *Coming of age in the 21st century: The lives and context of emerging adults* (pp. 117–134). Washington, D.C.: American Psychological Association.

Phinney, J., & Ong, A. (2007). Conceptualization and measurement of ethnic identity: Current status and future directions. *Journal of Counseling Psychology*, *54*(3), 271–281.

Phinney, J. S., Romero, I., Nava, M., & Huang, D. (2001). The role of language, parents, and peers in ethnic identity among adolescents in immigrant families. *Journal of Youth and Adolescence*, *30*(2), 135–153.

Phinney, J. S., & Rosenthal, D. (1992). Ethnic identity in adolescence: Process, context, and outcome. In T. Gulotta & R. Montemayor (Eds.), *Adolescent identity formation* (pp. 145–172). Newbury Park, CA: Sage Publications.

Portes, A. (1995). Segmented assimilation among new immigrant youth: A conceptual framework. In W. A. Cornelius & R. Rumbaut (Eds.), *California's immigrant children: Theory, research, and implications for educational policy* (pp. 71–76). San Diego, CA: University of California.

Portes, A., & Rumbaut, R. G. (2001). *Legacies: The story of the immigrant second generation.* Berkeley, CA: University of California Press.

Portes, A., & Rumbaut, R. G. (2006). *Immigrant America: A portrait*. (3rd ed.). Berkeley, CA: University of California Press.

Portes, A., & Zhou, M. (1993). The new second generation: Segmented assimilation and its variants. *Annals of the American Academy of Political and Social Science*, *530*, 74–96.

Quintana, S. M. (2007). Racial and ethnic identity: Developmental perspectives and research. *Journal of Counseling Psychology*, *54*(3), 259–270. doi:10.1037/0022–0167.54.3.259

Rodríguez, C. (2000). *Changing race*. New York, NY: New York University Press.

Rodríguez, C., & Cordero-Guzmán, H. (1992). Placing race in context. *Ethnic and Racial Studies*, *15*(4), 523–544.

Rumbaut, R. G. (1994). The crucible within: Ethnic identity, self-esteem, and segmented assimilation among children of immigrants. *International Migration Review*, *28*(4), 748–794.

Rumbaut, R. G. (1997). Ties that bind: Immigration and immigrant families in the United States. In A. Booth, A. C. Crouter, & N. S. Landale (Eds.), *Immigration and the family: Research and policy on U.S. immigrants* (pp. 3–46). Mahwah, NJ: Lawrence Erlbaum.

Rumbaut, R. G. (2000). Profiles in resilience: Educational achievement and ambition among children of immigrants in Southern California. In R. Taylor (Ed.), *Resilience across contexts: Family, work, culture, and community* (pp. 257–294). Mahwah, NJ: Lawrence Erlbaum.

Rumbaut, R. G., & Portes, A. (2001). *Ethnicities: Children of immigrants in American*. Berkeley, CA: University of California Press.

Rybas, N. (2012). Producing the self at the digital interface. In P. H. Cheong, J. N. Martin, & L. P. Macfadyen (Eds.), *New media and intercultural communication: Identity, community, and politics* (pp. 93–105). New York, NY: Peter Lang.

Saenz, R., Hwang, S. S., Aguirre, B. E., & Anderson, R. N. (1995). Persistence and change in Asian identity among children of intermarried couples. *Sociological Perspectives*, *38*(2), 175–194.

Sears, D. O., Fu, M., Henry, P. J., & Bui, K. (2003). The origins and persistence of ethnic identity among the "new immigrant" groups. *Social Psychology*, *66*(4), 419–437.

Shao, G. (2009). Understanding the appeal of user-generated media: A uses and gratification perspective. *Internet Research*, *19*(1), 7–25.

Song, A. M. (2003). *Choosing ethnic identity*. Cambridge, UK: Polity Press.

Syed, M., & Azmitia, M. (2009). Longitudinal trajectories of ethnic identity during the college years. *Journal of Research on Adolescence*, *19*(4), 601–624.

Tajfel, H. (1981). *Human groups and social categories*. Cambridge, UK: Cambridge University Press.

Tenenboim-Weinblatt, K. (2010). Producing identity: Introduction. In M. M. Kraidy & K. Sender (Eds.), *The politics of reality television: Global perspectives* (pp. 15–17). New York, NY: Routledge.

Teranishi, R. (2002). Asian Pacific Americans and critical race theory: An examination of school racial climate. *Equity and Excellence in Education*, *35*(2), 144–154.

Thai, H. C. (2002). Formation of ethnic identity among second-generation Vietnamese Americans. In P. G. Min (Ed.), *The second generation: Ethnic identity among Asian Americans* (pp. 53–83). Walnut Creek, CA: AltaMira Press.

Thomas, M. (2011). *Deconstructing digital natives: Young people, technology, and the new literacies*. New York, NY: Routledge.

Tomlinson, J. (1999). *Globalization and culture*. Chicago, IL: The University of Chicago Press.

Tuan, M. (1998). Neither *real* Americans nor *real* Asians? Multigeneration Asian ethnics navigating the terrain of authenticity. *Qualitative Sociology*, *22*(2), 105–125.

United States Census Bureau. (2015). *American Community Survey (ACS)*. Retrieved from https://www.census.gov/programs-surveys/acs/data.html

Umaña-Taylor, A. J. (2004). Ethnic identity and self-esteem: Examining the role of social context. *Journal of Adolescence*, *27*(2), 139–146.

Valkenburg, P. M., & Peter, J. (2009). The effects of instant messaging on the quality of adolescents' existing friendships: A longitudinal study. *Journal of Communication*, *59*, 79–97.

van den Berghe, P. L. (1978). Race and ethnicity: A sociobiological perspective. *Ethnic and Racial Studies*, *1*(4), 401–411.

Waggoner, D. (1988). Language minorities in the United States in the 1980s: The evidence from the 1980 census. In S. McKay & S. C. Wong (Eds.), *Language diversity: Problem or resource? A social and educational perspective on language minorities in the United States* (pp. 69–108). New York, NY: Newbury House.

Wakefield, W. D., & Hudley, C. (2007). Ethnic and racial identity and adolescent well-being. *Theories into Practice*, *46*(2), 147–154.

Waldinger, R., & Fitzgerald, D. (2004). Transnationalism in question. *American Journal of Sociology*, *109*(5), 1177–1195.

Warner, W. L., & Srole, L. (1945). *The social systems of American ethnic groups*. New Haven, CT: Yale University Press.

Waters, M. C. (1990). *Ethnic options: Choosing identities in America*. Berkeley, CA: University of California Press.

Waters, M. C. (1999). *Black identities: West Indian immigrant dreams and American realities*. New York, NY: Russell Sage Foundation Books at Harvard University Press.

Yang, P. (2012). Who am I in virtual space? A dialectical approach to students' online identity expression. In P. H. Cheong, J. N. Martin, & L. P. Macfadyen (Eds.), *New media and intercultural communication: Identity, community, and politics* (pp. 109–121). New York, NY: Peter Lang.

Yi, Y. (2009). Adolescent literacy and identity construction among 1.5 generation students: From a transnational perspective. *Journal of Asian Pacific Communication*, *19*(1), 100–129.

Yoon, E. (2011). Measuring ethnic identity in the Ethnic Identity Scale and the Multigroup Ethnic Identity Measure–Revised. *Cultural Diversity & Ethnic Minority Psychology*, *17*(2), 144–155.

Zhou, M. (1997). Segmented assimilation: Issues, controversies, and recent research on the new second generation. *International Migration Review, 31*(4), 975–1008.

Zhou, M., & Bankston III, C. L. (1994). Social capital and the adaptation of the second generation: The case of Vietnamese youth in New Orleans. *International Migration Review,* 28(4), 775–799.

Zou, Y., & Trueba, E. (Eds.). (1998). *Ethnic identity and power: Cultural contexts of political action in school and society*. New York, NY: State University of New York Press.

# · 2 ·

# STUDYING KOREAN AMERICAN YOUTH

## Being Korean American

According to the 2015 Census, Asian Americans belong to the fastest growing ethnic group in the U.S. from 2000 to 2015. Korean Americans comprise a large segment of the Asian American population in the U. S., with a total of 1.8 million among the entire U.S. population identifying themselves as Korean descent (U.S. Census Bureau, 2015).

Within the Korean American community, an immigrant Korean family is recognized as a family that speaks primarily Korean at home, eats Korean food, emphasizes the values of filial piety, has predominantly Korean friends, and celebrates Korean holidays (Danico, 2004). According to Hurh (1998) and Min (1995), Korean Americans maintain a high level of ethnicity compared to other Asian American minority groups. While Korean Americans are outwardly becoming assimilated in the U.S. society, they are inwardly continuing to retain their traditional ethnic heritage (Min, 1995).

The classification "first generation parents" refers to adult immigrants who were born in Korea and arrived in the new country after reaching adulthood. "First-and-a-half generation children" refers to those who were born in Korea and were generally between 11 and 16 years of age at the time of immigration with their family, possess memories of life in Korea, are able to speak both conversational Korean and English, become consciously dual-oriented, and are capable of blending Korean and American ethnic expressions (Danico, 2004, pp. 5–6). "Second generation children" refers to their American-born or American-raised children (Kim & Yu, 1996), and 1.8 generation refers to those who were born in Korea and moved with their parents to the U.S. before the age of 11, as they are similar in characteristics to the second generation Korean Americans (Danico, 2004). Most prominently, second generation children of Korean Americans make up one growing portion of this population. Unlike their immigrant parents, who, in many ways, remain tied to their countries of origin, these children are raised in America, attend American schools, and are expected to become integral members of society (Portes & Rumbaut, 2001). As second generation Korean American children are a crucial and permanent part of American society, understanding the impact of immigration on these children, their overall patterns of adaptation, as well as their ethnic identity formation is particularly important because the future of this young population will be determined by the different forms of social adaptation they experience, which will also have a profound impact on American society.

The second generation children of Korean immigrants in the U.S. often find themselves caught between two different cultural worlds since they are born of Korean parents on American soil. They are American citizens by birth, but Koreans by blood (Kwon & Kim, 1993). The children grow up as Americans, and they quickly become fully equipped with the language and cultural knowhow because of their regular contact with non-Korean children at school that exposes them to mainstream culture (Lehrer, 1996). Since they are more familiar with American culture than their parents (Kibria, 2002; Portes & Rumbaut, 2005), they realize that their parents' culture is different from that of their American friends. Such children of first generation Korean immigrants often experience the sense of being different from their local peers in terms of skin color and become ashamed that their parents are different from those of their peers (Akhtar, 2011). Distinct differences between their home culture and culture-at-large force these children to float insecurely between two worlds without a definite feeling of belonging to either group (Bandon, 1994).

An example of the differing rate of acculturation among Korean immigrants is the division that exists between traditional parents and their rapidly acculturating children. While their parents grew up in Korea and came to America after their cultural orientations were already fixed, the second generation grew up in the American social-cultural environment. Parents are trying to adapt to the different social norms that value autonomy and independence, while at the same time they often would like to preserve traditional values, such as maintaining the family's public face (Shim, Kim, & Martin, 2008). However, second generation children consider themselves more American than Korean and feel no need to learn the culture of their parents' country (Bandon, 1994). Indeed, in the eyes of parents, their children's reluctance to learn Korean language and culture indicates a lack of respect for them and their ethnic backgrounds (Lehrer, 1996).

The second generation, unlike the first and first-and-a-half generations, inherits all of the basic legal rights that come with being an "American," including the capacity to run for President. More importantly, they have an inherent sense of their Korean American identity (Lehrer, 1996). For them, English and American culture are primary, while the Korean language and culture are secondary. Then, at a certain point, they also realize they are not "truly" Americans in many ways, including in their looks and life values (Park, 2009). In other words, although they have grown up as Americans, there are differences and uncertainties in their identities compared to their American friends. In this context, they cannot fully identify with their parents or their American friends. Thus, second generation children go through a kind of identity struggle related to their racial ethnicity. While some become rapidly assimilated into mainstream White society, some embrace their parents' ethnic identity (Kim & Kim, 1994). According to Min and Kim (1999), many U.S.-born Asian American children identify themselves as Americans when they are young; however, as they grow older, they increasingly choose their parents' ethnic identity as their own.

Regarding having a very different background compared to their parents, Park (2009) argues that second generation children show very different acculturation processes in contrast to those of their parents (first generation Korean immigrants). According to her study, the acculturation processes of second generation children are in fact acculturation to the "Korean American" ethnic group and de-acculturation from "Americans." This is in contrast to their parents, where acculturation means becoming "American." Second generation children grow up becoming assimilated into the society, but when they reach the age when cultural identities emerge as something significant in their lives, they experience a new adaptation process. Although they are first enculturated into American society, they eventually experience acculturation during adolescence. Park (2009) used the new term "re-acculturation," or the process of becoming acculturated back into the originating ethnic group since it means going back to being "Korean American" from "American" (p. 80).

Unlike immigrants who maintain the status of being first generation, the first-and-a-half generation (technically first generation) is seen with much less specificity. The basic characteristics of "first-and-a-half generation Korean Americans" are generally recognized as bi-cultural and bilingual individuals who are neither first nor second generation immigrants (Hurh, 1998; Koh, 1994; Ryu, 1991). The first generation views them as second generation immigrants, the second generation conversely perceives them as first generation immigrants, and non-Koreans see them as just ambiguous or simply "Korean" (Danico, 2004, p. 24).

Even though scholars have different ways of describing the first-and-a-half generation, they all acknowledge that there are significantly noticeable differences between first-and-a-half generation and second generation children in terms of their psychological developmental stages, their social relations and activities, as well as their orientation toward their country of origin. Kim (1977) indicates that a young age at the time of immigration is expected to result in greater assimilation because younger children are more likely to adapt more quickly to a new country and culture.

When young Korean children migrate to the U.S. with their family, they bring with them their Koreanness. In this regard, at the time of immigration, the sense of identity among these children is Korean (Gwak, 2008). However, in the U.S., they naturally experience a process of re-socialization, where they are exposed to various external influences and introduced to the cultures, values, and norms of the host society. In other words, they arrive at the U.S. with a sense of a Korean identity, but throughout the course of their life, they are expected to assimilate into American society. During the process of their re-socialization in the U.S., the individual's sense of ethnic identity transforms due to sociocultural experiences and external influences that eventually contribute to the negotiation and expression of their ethnic identities as they accommodate new cultures and values (Danico, 2004, p. 12). At the same time, they are inevitably exposed to Korean influences from their families because the passing of Koreaness, from speaking Korean, to eating Korean food, and to socializing with co-ethnics at home, is reinforced by their parents (p. 13). Such children may lean more in one direction or the other, but they demonstrate flexible bi-cultural orientation and are able to synthesize their two different cultural elements into their ethnic identities (Akhtar, 2011). Therefore, first-and-a-half generation Korean Americans are defined here as those who are generally between 11 and 16 years of age at the time of immigration with their family, possess their memories of life in Korea, are able to speak both conversational Korean and English, become consciously dual-oriented, and are capable of blending Korean and American ethnic expressions (Danico, 2004, pp. 5–6).

## Confucianism in the Korean American Family

It is difficult to discuss Korean immigrant families without examining the influence of Confucianism on them. As a peninsula located in the heart of northeastern Asia, Korea's geographical proximity to China created a cultural link between the two countries (Yum, 1987). Unlike in the U.S., Confucianism has historically functioned almost like a national religion, which regulates morals, ethics, and social orders in Korea, and has become the cornerstone of Korean culture (Hurh, 1998). While dictated by the influence of Confucianism, Korean culture is also significantly affected by collectivism, which does not consider individuals as independent entities, but as parts of the group as a whole. Hui and Triandis (1986) defined collectivistic cultures as those where: (1) more emphasis is placed on the consequences of one's actions for others in the community than in individualistic cultures, (2) a person is part of the community's life, (3) group harmony is emphasized, (4) a person's behavior is more likely to be controlled by shame, (5) the consequences of a person's actions, whether they are good or bad, are shared by all, and (6) resources are shared. This collectivistic culture results in the belief that the actions of one person affect the rest of the community, particularly the family. Therefore, duties, obligations, and decisions are shared as a whole.

One fundamental difference between the Korean and American family systems derives from two oppositional sets of family values: filial piety-centered Confucian collectivism, with its priority on family interest, mutual interdependence, and obligation, versus conjugal love-centered American individualism, with its emphasis on individual interests, rights, and independence (Hurh, 1998, pp. 83–84). In contrast to the collectivistic culture of Korea, families migrating to the U.S. are introduced to an individualistic culture. Family members in the U.S. are expected to be independent, autonomous, and self-reliant, which is the opposite of the interdependent mindset of Korean culture (Nisbett, 2003). In general, Korean American parents carry significantly different cultural beliefs, values, and parenting practices that are under the strong influence of Confucianism than American parents, which may influence parent-child interactions (Kim & Choi, 1994). With the traditional belief that the children are to be extensions of the parents, Korean American parents assume full responsibilities for their children's behaviors and outcomes. This responsibility, with the belief that they know what's best for their children, leads to parents being extensively involved in making decisions in their children's lives (Nisbett, 2003, p. 58). Thus, the virtues of filial piety, family loyalty, and strict obedience to parents are still regarded as the norm that Korean descendants do not find among their American peers' families (Lehrer, 1996).

One particular area in which Korean Americans are well-known is their educational attainment in that they are well represented in the nation's colleges and universities (Lehrer, 1996). Influenced by Confucian beliefs, Korean parents regard their children's education as the single most important contributor to future success; therefore, they take extraordinary efforts to ensure that their children have every opportunity to obtain the best education (Kim & Kim, 1994). Why did Korean immigrants leave everything they knew behind and decide to come to the U.S.? One of the most important motivations for Korean immigrants to immigrate to the U.S. was to provide a better education for their children (Hurh, 1998). Today, Korean American parents are intimately involved in their children's academic performance and often demand a discipline and dedication based upon Confucianism unfamiliar to most American families (Lehrer, 1996). In addition, Korean parents expect their children to master not only the American curriculum, but to also attend special Korean schools that teach Korean language and customs (Lehrer, 1996). Positioned between two conflicting cultural forces, the children of Korean immigrants in the U.S. may be more or less individualistic or collectivistic, depending on the context or situation. For example, one may behave more collectively with one's family and more individualistically in one's school. Korean Americans' unique hybridized cultural atmosphere provides a platform to understand how the children of Korean immigrants in the U.S. can maintain cultural orientations that infuse elements of contrasting values—such as individualism and collectivism. Thus, the children of Korean immigrants in the U.S. function in some respects more like Koreans at some times and more like Americans at other times (Nisbett, 2003). Because they are often able to view cultures alternately as if through different pairs of eyes, the children of Korean immigrants in the U.S. can suggest new ways of thinking about America and different ways of being American.

## The Korean Wave: *Hallyu*

The free circulation of popular culture across national boundaries is increasingly facilitating new links among youths around the world (Ju, 2007). For example, popular culture consumption, such as watching Korean TV dramas and listening to Korean popular music (hereafter referred to as K-pop), is a significant part of youths' leisure activities (Kim, 2009). In other words, the global consumption of popular culture has become another distinct social element of the young generation, and digital media have become an efficient and simple way to promote this consumption (Kim & Kim, 2011).

In the mid-1990s, Beijing journalists began using the term "Korean Wave" (*Hallyu* in Korean) to describe the unprecedented surge in popularity of Korean popular culture throughout China (Hogarth, 2013, p. 136). Following this initial boom of Korean popular culture in China, the Korean Wave rapidly won over legions of fans in other Asian countries. In the growing international spread of popular culture products from Korea, the Korean Wave even impacted the Middle East, Europe, Africa, and the Americas, far beyond the boundaries of Asia (Lee, 2007). *The Seattle Times* summarized the impact of the Korean Wave as penetrating beyond Asia with pop music, TV dramas, and films that dazzle audiences from Tokyo and Beijing all the way to Seattle (Dickie, 2006).

Korean television dramas, including soap operas and fictional miniseries, have become the major factor behind the unexpected popularity of the Korean Wave in many Asian countries, such as Cambodia, China, Hong Kong, Japan, Taiwan, and Thailand. The major Asian and Asian American communities in California, New York, Chicago, and the Washington, D.C. area also played an increasingly visible role in the proliferation of Korean popular culture. With advanced digital technologies, online versions of these dramas became available for little or no cost and with various subtitle options, including English, Japanese, Thai, Indonesian, Turkish, Spanish, and several Chinese dialects (Jung, 2009).

With their combination of engaging narratives, fully-developed characters, and sophisticated visual styles, Korean TV dramas are considered some of the best TV productions in the world (Hogarth, 2013). According to a *Chicago Sun-Times* columnist in May of 2004, "U.S. audiences for Korean television dramas are small, but vocal and devoted. Stations in Chicago, Philadelphia, Honolulu, Los Angeles, Seattle, Washington, and New York offer several shows daily. These cities have sizable Korean-American populations, but Korean-Americans are not the sole audience" (D'Alessio, 2004). Despite fans' testimonials, the question remains: what are the main reasons for the success of Korean TV dramas among Asians and Asian Americans around the world? According to *The New York Times*, Korean TV dramas are regarded as more emotionally engaging and powerful because of the dramatic stories that often enable all viewers, including women and men as well as the young and the old, to feel emotionally invested (Onishi, 2005). For example, these dramas deal with a wide range of stories, from depictions of family matters and relationships to historical dramas (e.g., *Daejangeum*, *Jumong*, and *Emperor of the Sea*) and to the most popular types of stories, most notably romance (e.g., *Autumn Fairy Tale*, *Winter Sonata*, and *Boys over Flowers*) (Kim & Kim, 2011). Regarding the significance of the characters in these dramas, women are portrayed as strong, independent-minded, and high-principled individuals with the courage of their convictions and who overcome difficulties even in dire circumstances, while men are often depicted as gentle, romantic, caring lovers and fathers, and sometimes doting husbands (Hogarth, 2013). Beyond the characters, the popularity of Korean TV dramas can also be attributed to their filtering of Western values through Korea's own production style and unique repository of narratives (Ju, 2007).

K-pop is another important cultural product, characterized by slick dance routines, catchy American pop-influenced melodies, and the physical attractiveness of its performers (Tudor, 2012). Interestingly, K-pop is not based solely on traditional Korean song and dance, but rather on combinations of local and foreign elements at multiple levels (Hogarth, 2013). Its strong beats mixed with its unique rhythms have appealed to the musical and visual sensibilities of numerous teenagers all over the world. One particularly interesting feature that separates K-pop from other music industries is that K-pop groups have much larger numbers, ranging from the usual five members to as many as 13.

As a result of the Korean Wave, a visible circulation of Korean popular culture products, from fashion to music and to television dramas, has impacted everyday lives in the U.S. (Huat & Iwabuchi, 2008), where the effect of the Korean Wave has positively and significantly improved not only the image and prestige of Korean popular culture but also the images of resident Korean Americans (Kim & Kim, 2011). The Korean Wave is therefore celebrated through a lens of national triumph and regarded as a valuable vehicle for spreading both Korean culture and Korean ethnic identity (Ju, 2007). In this context, as digital technology innovations give people around the world new means to consume Korean popular culture, the intersection of digital media, the Korean Wave, and the improved image of Korea in general pose intriguing questions about whether and how these factors give the children of Korean immigrants more power in constructing and expressing their evolving ethnic identities on the internet (Kim, 2009; Yang, 2012).

## The Study

This study investigates the realities—due to the marginalization of the ethnic community in the broader host society—of younger generation Korean Americans' ongoing negotiations and expressions of their ethnic identities in the context of digital media technologies and interrogates the role of digital media in these online communications and encounters. More specifically, as stated in the introduction, we ask: What is the nature of the digital media practices of children of Korean immigrants in the U.S. in their socialization and in the development of their ethnic identity? How do they engage in the exploration of and commitment to their ethnic identity using the digital media devices at their disposal? How does digital media consumption affect this young population's assimilation into mainstream American society? To learn about the role of digital media in the lives of Korean American children, we employed a combination of two methods: interviews elicited by photos and a survey.

This study primarily relies on qualitative research methods, with further support coming in the form of a quantitative survey. According to McMillan (2004) and LeCompte and Preissle (1993), qualitative research methods are specifically designed to provide a wealth of detailed information described by the interviewees, with the latter explaining how they are therefore best suited to research that investigates the multiple "dynamic realities" of interviewees' experiences (LeCompte & Preissle, 1993, p. 47). Indeed, one distinct advantage of qualitative research techniques is their ability to extract and expose the multiple realities represented in interviewees' perspectives (McMillan, 2004). As McMillan (2004) further emphasizes, qualitative researchers need to reconstruct what is actually going on in the sphere of life under study based on the subjects' views of their own world.

Among the qualitative research techniques available, photo-elicitation interview (PEI) is selected as the instrument for this study. PEI is a type of qualitative, inquiry-based research that enhances the interview by allowing either researchers to use photographs as a tool to expand on questions or interviewees to use them as a means to present their experiences, beliefs, perspectives, and understanding of their worlds (Clark-Ibáñez, 2004). As Harper (2002) describes PEIs, while photographs can provide researchers with a semi-structured interview, they can also sharpen interviewees' memories to recall deeper elements of information from them. Also, photographs can improve the interview experience with children by lessening some areas of misunderstanding because they act as a focal point, particularly in cases of using photographs taken by children who are more familiar with the image contexts (Clark-Ibáñez, 2004). Compared to other data collection techniques, in which the researcher usually has a certain idea of what he or she wants to find out, PEI is a discovery-oriented technique that instead allows the interviewee to take photographic images and manage what he or she wants to share with the interviewer using those photos. Because this project aims to explore the complexity of ethnic identity formation among young Korean American children who are caught between two different cultures, PEIs will provide these young interviewees with a clear, tangible prompt in order to better help the researcher explore and glean information about their perceptions and lived realities.

However, Phinney (1996) claims that although interviews are the most effective tools for studying how individuals move through ethnic identity developmental stages, they are unwieldy and inefficient for examining large-scale population trends. She therefore recommends using questionnaires and surveys as alternative methods of uncovering information about ethnic identity development in large populations, arguing that surveys and questionnaires that treat ethnic identity as a "continuous variable" are very useful tools for large-scale research on ethnic identity (Phinney, 1996, p. 148). While the qualitative technique emphasizes the "multiple subjective views" of the people involved in the events, a quantitative measure is generally used for providing an "objective truth of factual events" (Roth & Mehta, 2002, p. 137). For example, in the case of McMillan's (2004) research, which employed a number of methods to examine unskilled female laborers' perceptions of television advertising in India, it was documented that the combination of the quantitative survey method and the qualitative ethnographic method demonstrated synergy because interviewees were given the chance to explain their survey responses during individual interviews, thereby resulting in "data that were rich in depth as well as breadth" (pp. 501–502). Therefore, the present research design combined qualitative PEIs with surveys of young Korean Americans in the U.S. to accommodate large populations.

*Photo-elicited interviews (PEI)*: 31 interviewees were recruited through snowball sampling (Lindlof & Taylor, 2011) of youths in Korean churches in a small rural university town (referred to as Rural, in the text) and a large city in the Midwest (referred to as City), as well as in a metropolitan area on the west coast (referred to as Metro), all of which have significant Korean American populations. At the time of the interviews, between May and August of 2013, the interviewees' ages ranged from 13 to 18 years old, and their length of residence in the U.S. ranged from 4 to 15 years. They were asked during an introductory meeting to take 10 to 15 photographs using their mobile devices that represented their regular media practices and important images or symbols in their lives as immigrant children in the U.S. They were further requested to include a memo about each subject they photographed (see Appendix A). According to Schwartz (1989), photographs can elucidate that which the interviewee takes for granted and which the researcher has possibly never considered. After obtaining all the pictures, semi-structured PEIs were arranged with each interviewee.

During the interviews that followed, in the participants' homes or churches, they were asked about their background and personal history. Looking at the photos together with the interviewer, they then discussed in English and/or Korean (whichever was more comfortable, with many interviews flowing back and forth between the two languages) the thoughts and feelings they evoked. Since the photos were taken by the interviewees in their own unique social/cultural worlds, each knows his or her photograph and was able to both communicate his or her own visual voice through each photo and expand upon them in own words in the interviews. Becker (1986) and Schwartz (1989) argue that these "auto-driven photographs" have the potential to reveal multiple meanings in the viewing process, provide insight into the interviewees' first-hand experiences, facilitate discussions between the interviewer and interviewee, and uncover interviewees' interpretations of material reality. In this process, a dialogue was created in which the typical research roles were reversed. The researcher became the listener and the one who encouraged the dialogue to continue. The interviewees themselves were able to make statements about their social or cultural world and express matters of the heart and mind through the photos they took. The picture and words together formed a meaningful package to help the researcher understand the interviewees' digital media practices and their perceptions about issues regarding their ethnic identity. To maintain anonymity, the interviewer used pseudonyms for each interviewee when reporting the findings. For example, interviewees who go by Korean names were given English pseudonyms, while interviewees who instead go by English names were given Korean pseudonyms.

The interviews lasted between an hour and an hour and a half and were audio-recorded and fully transcribed into written documents as is conventional in qualitative studies (Lindlof & Taylor, 2011). The Korean identity of the interviewer (the first author) facilitated a sense of comfort, familiarity, and trust. Her position as both insider and outsider in American society as well as other dimensions of her social identity as a young Korean woman came to the foreground and permeated the entire research process. When hearing their stories, the researcher's sense of self as an ethnic minority was deeply connected to that of the informants, who are caught between two different cultural worlds in the fabric of their lives. However, having a sense of camaraderie challenged the researcher to constantly negotiate the intricate boundary between being the researcher and the researched.

During the analytic process, we immersed ourselves in the interviewees' responses in order to listen to their voices and remain free from judgment. One of the particular challenges associated with interpreting qualitative data is that the data is inherently unstructured (LeCompte, 2000), making it the researcher's responsibility to derive structure from the patterns that emerge in the data analysis. According to Huberman and Miles (1998), the work of qualitative data analysis is characterized both by inductive and deductive approaches. The former aims at inferring "a principle from many particulars of discourse and action," whereas the latter is used to test "that principle by subjecting it to new instances of discourse and action" (Lindlof & Taylor, 2011, p. 243). While the researcher using the inductive approach analyzes the codes that emerge from the data, the researcher using deductive analysis codes the data according to the theoretical framework that he or she established while framing the questions. In order to improve the validity of the outcomes, Huberman and Miles (1998) also suggest performing data analysis through repeated cycles in which the researcher probes the data several times by employing various techniques to apply existing codes and discover new codes (p. 186). Therefore, each transcript from the interviews was read, re-read, and coded for emerging categories for thematic analysis.

In this study, the deductive codes were "digital media" and "ethnic identity," while the inductive codes emerged around the issues of digital media and ethnic identity. Regarding the latter, we followed the recommendation by LeCompte (2000) that an analysis of frequency, or noticing items that emerge repeatedly across interviewees, reveals important inductive codes. Indeed, the codes in this study tended to emerge either through interviewees' declarations or through an analysis of frequency. Declarations were particularly important in the identification of differing cases, in which some participants disagreed with items to which other participants frequently made reference. Also, declarations tended to feed analyses of frequency. More specifically, in the interest of engaging in a research cycle that is both iterative yet revealing, the researcher would transcribe, code, and review coded interviews during data collection. Through this review, themes and items about which participants made declarations were noted, and further questions about these declarations were then inserted into other interviewees' interviews.

After coding the interviews, Huberman and Miles' (1998) thirteen tactics for generating meaning from data were used to structure the data in a way that clarified the relationships between codes (p. 187), tactics which fall into three separate categories. The first includes tactics for developing and elucidating codes: observing patterns and themes, seeing plausibility, clustering, making metaphors, counting, making contrasts and comparisons, and partitioning variables. The second involves tactics for observing the data more abstractly: bringing particulars into general categories, factoring, observing relations between variables, and looking for intervening variables. The final category includes those tactics that contribute to a comprehensive understanding of the data and allow the researcher to draw conclusions: building a logical chain of evidence and making conceptual and theoretical coherence.

During the analytic process, our goal was to lose ourselves in the interviewees' responses in order to listen to their voices and remain free from judgment. While the researchers went back and forth among the interviews, some data did begin to cluster into areas rich enough to produce emerging common themes that could characterize the ways the interviewees use their digital media devices and their ethnic identity exploration or commitment associated with them.

*Survey:* The use of a questionnaire complemented this approach and allowed for a systematic study of a much larger population, validating the PEI findings and allowing for generalizability. The survey included multiple-choice questions about participants' digital media devices, frequency of use, media content preferences, level of engagement with SNSs, and so forth. In addition, questions investigating their language use as well as demographic questions were added to the survey. Finally, ethnic identity measure questions that assess individuals' degree of identity exploration, level of commitment, participation in ethnic cultural activities, and affirmation and belonging regarding their ethnic group were included (i.e., the Multigroup Ethnic Identity Measure–Revised [MEIM–R]; Phinney & Ong, 2007) (See Appendix B).

A different group of participants were recruited during the month of August, 2013 through Korean churches in a large metropolitan area on the west coast. In total, 154 youths of Korean descent completed the paper-based survey, their ages ranging from 14 to 18 years old (mean age of 15.7) and their length of residence in the U.S. ranging from 4 to 16 years. The sample was proportionately even between 78 males (50.7%) and 76 females (49.3%). Of the 154 participants, 88 (57%) were born in Korea and 66 (43%) were born in the U.S. In terms of generation status, 66 (42.9%) participants who were born in the U.S. are clearly second generation Korean Americans. 88 (57.1%) were born in Korea, but some of them migrated at such a young age that they were grouped into the second generation as well, as defined earlier in the discussion above. At the end, 28 participants (18.2%) were defined as first-and-a-half generation and 126 participants (81.8%) as second generation. Therefore, the vast majority of the participants in this study, both males and females, were second generation Korean Americans. Completion took between 15 and 20 minutes on average, with each participant receiving $5 for completing the survey.

The quantitative data collected through the questionnaires was analyzed using SPSS software. The descriptive data of the questions were also available according to gender, age, and basic demographic variables. Furthermore, in order to examine the correlation between the various aspects of participants' digital media practices and ethnic identity construction, statistical analyses, including descriptive statistics (e.g., frequencies and cross-tabs) for describing the sample and the main variables, and reliability analyses were performed.

Together, the findings from the PEI interviews and the survey provided a rich body of information about the role of digital media in the construction of Korean American youths' hybrid identities. The presentation of the findings was organized around several major themes that emerged from the interviews in Chapters Three through Six, and the major theoretical discussions will be covered in the final chapter. All of the photos and statements in this section were used with the authorization of interviewees and their parents, and, as previously stated, interviewees were given pseudonyms to protect their identity.

We turn now to exploring these findings.

## References

Akhtar, S. (2011). *Immigration and acculturation: Mourning, adaptation, and the next generation.* Lanham, MD: Jason Aronson.

Bandon, A. (1994). *Korean Americans.* New York, NY: New Discovery.

Becker, H. S. (1986). *Doing things together: Selected papers.* Evanston, IL: Northwestern University Press.

Clark-Ibáñez, M. (2004). Framing the social world with photo-elicitation interviews. *American Behavioral Scientist, 47*(12), 1507–1527.

D'Alessio, F. N. (2004, May 4). American fans hooked on Korean soaps. *Chicago Sun-Times*. Retrieved from https://www.highbeam.com/doc/1P2-1531730.html

Danico, M. Y. (2004). *The 1.5 generation: Becoming Korean American in Hawaii*. Honolulu, HI: University of Hawaii Press.

Dickie, L. (2006, June 4). The Korean wave. *The Seattle Times*. Retrieved from http://old.seattletimes.com/html/opinion/2003036091_sundaykorea04.html

Gwak, S. (2008). *Be(com)ing Korean in the United States: Exploring ethnic identity formation through cultural practices*. Amherst, NY: Cambria Press.

Harper, D. (2002). Talking about pictures: A case for photo elicitation. *Visual Studies, 17*(1), 13–26.

Hogarth, H. K. (2013). The Korean wave: An Asian reaction to western-dominated globalization. *Perspectives on Global Development and Technology, 12*, 135–151.

Huat, C. B., & Iwabuchi, K. (Eds.). (2008). *East Asian pop culture: Analysing the Korean wave*. Hong Kong: Hong Kong University Press.

Huberman, A. M., & Miles, M. (1998). Data management and analysis methods. In N. Denzin & Y. Lincoln (Eds.), *Collecting and interpreting qualitative materials* (pp. 179–210). Thousand Oaks, CA: Sage Publications.

Hui, C. H., & Triandis, H. C. (1986). Individualism and collectivism: A study of cross-cultural researchers. *Journal of Cross-Cultural Psychology, 17*(2), 225–248.

Hurh, W. M. (1993). The 1.5 generation: A cornerstone of the Korean-American ethnic community. In H. Kwon & S. Kim (Eds.), *The emerging generation of Korean-Americans* (pp. 47–79). Seoul: Kyung Hee University Press.

Hurh, W. M. (1998). *The Korean Americans*. Westport, CT: Greenwood Press.

Ju, H. (2007). The nature of nationalism in the "Korean wave": A framing analysis of news coverage about Korean pop culture. In *Conference Papers—National Communication Association* (Vol. 1).

Jung, E.-Y. (2009). Transnational Korea: A critical assessment of the Korean wave in Asia and the United States. *Southeast Review of Asian Studies, 31*, 69–80.

Kibria, N. (2002). *Becoming Asian American: Second generation Chinese and Korean American identities*. Baltimore, MD: Johns Hopkins University Press.

Kim, D. K., & Kim, M.-S. (Eds.). (2011). *Hallyu: Influence of Korean popular culture in Asia and beyond*. Seoul: Seoul National University Press.

Kim, E. H., & Yu, E. Y. (1996). *East to America: Korean American life stories*. New York, NY: The New York Press.

Kim, H. (1977). *The Korean diaspora: Historical and sociological studies of Korean immigration and assimilation in North America*. Santa Barbara, CA: ABC-Clio.

Kim, L. I., & Kim, G. S. (1994). *Korean American immigrants and their children*. San Francisco, CA: Many Cultures Publisher.

Kim, U., & Choi, S. (1994). Individualism, collectivism, and child development: A Korean perspective. In P. Greenfield & R. Cocking (Eds.), *Cross-cultural roots of minority child development* (pp. 227–257). Hillsdale, NJ: Lawrence Erlbaum.

Kim, Y. (2009). *Media consumption and everyday life in Asia*. London: Routledge.

Koh, T. H. (1994). Ethnic identity in first, 1.5, and second generation Korean Americans: An exploratory study. In H. Y. Kwon (Ed.), *Korean Americans: Conflict and harmony* (pp. 43–53). Chicago, IL: North Park College.

Kwon, H. Y., & Kim, S. (1993). *The emerging generation of Korean Americans*. Seoul: Kyung Hee University Press.

LeCompte, M. (2000). Analyzing Qualitative Data. *Theory into Practice*, 39(3), 146–154.

LeCompte, M., & Preissle, J. (1993). *Ethnography and qualitative design in educational research*. (2nd ed.). San Diego, CA: Academic Press.

Lee, O. (2007). Does the Korean wave bring about country-of-origin effect? *Journal of Korea Trade*, 32(5), 405–426.

Lehrer, B. (1996). *The Korean Americans*. New York, NY: Chelsea House.

Lindlof, T. R., & Taylor, B. C. (2011). *Qualitative communication research methods*. (3rd ed.). Thousand Oaks, CA: Sage Publications.

McMillan, J. (2004). *Educational research: Fundamentals for the consumer* (4th ed.). Boston, MA: Pearson Education.

Min, P. G. (1995). *Asian Americans: Contemporary trends and issues*. Thousand Oaks, CA: Sage Publications.

Min, P. G., & Kim, R. (1999). *Struggle for ethnic identity: Narratives by Asian American professionals*. Walnut Creek, CA: AltaMira Press.

Nisbett, R. E. (2003). *The geography of thought: How Asians and Westerners think differently … and why*. New York, NY: Free Press.

Onishi, N. (2005, November 19). Ugly images of Asian rivals become best sellers in Japan. *New York Times*. Retrieved from http://www.nytimes.com/2005/11/19/world/asia/ugly-images-of-asian-rivals-become-best-sellers-in-japan.html

Park, S. (2009). Negotiating identities and re-acculturation of second-generation Korean Americans: The role of ethnic media and peer group dynamics. *Korea Journal*, 49(1), 61–97.

Phinney, J. (1996). Understanding ethnic diversity: The role of ethnic identity. *American Behavior Scientist*, 40(2), 143–152.

Phinney, J., & Ong, A. (2007). Conceptualization and measurement of ethnic identity: Current status and future directions. *Journal of Counseling Psychology*, 54(3), 271–281.

Portes, A., & Rumbaut, R. G. (2001). *Legacies: The story of the immigrant second generation*. Berkeley, CA: University of California Press.

Portes, A., & Rumbaut, R. G. (2005). Introduction: The second generation and the children of immigrants longitudinal study. *Ethnic and Racial Studies*, 28(6), 983–999.

Roth, W. D., & Mehta, J. D. (2002). The Rashomon effect: Combining positivist and interpretivist approaches in the analysis of contested events. *Sociological Methods & Research*, *31*(2), 131–173.

Ryu, C. (1991). 1.5 Generation. In J. F. J. Lee (Ed.), *Asian American experiences in the United States: Oral histories of first to fourth generation of Americans from China, Philippines, Japan, India, the Pacific Islands, Vietnam and Cambodia* (pp. 50–54). Jefferson, NC: McFarland & Company.

Shim, T. Y., Kim, M., & Martin, J. N. (2008). *Changing Korea: Understanding culture and communication*. New York, NY: Peter Lang.

Schwartz, D. (1989). Visual ethnography: Using photography in qualitative research. *Qualitative Sociology*, *12*(2), 119–153.

Tudor, D. (2012). *Korea: The impossible country*. North Clarendon, VT: Tuttle Publishing.

U.S. Census Bureau. (2015). *Asian/Pacific American Heritage Month: May 2015*. Retrieved from https://www.census.gov/newsroom/facts-for-features/2015/cb15-ff07.html

Yang, P. (2012). Who am I in virtual space? A dialectical approach to students' online identity expression. In P. H. Cheong, J. N. Martin, & L. P. Macfadyen (Eds.), *New media and intercultural communication: Identity, community, and politics* (pp. 109–121). New York, NY: Peter Lang.

Yum, J. O. (1987). Korean philosophy and communication. In D. L. Kincaid (Ed.), *Communication theory: Eastern and Western perspectives* (pp. 71–86). San Diego, CA: Academic Press.

# · 3 ·

# DIGITAL PRACTICES OF KOREAN AMERICAN YOUTH

We start with a discussion of the first research question of this study: What is the nature of the digital media practices of first-and-a-half and second generation descendants of Korean immigrants in their socialization processes and in the development of their ethnic identity?

The findings presented in this chapter demonstrate that on one hand, there is no significant difference between the digital practices of Korean American youth, in comparison to other immigrant youth, and non-immigrant youth. Digital media are deeply integrated in their everyday lives, with smartphones becoming the most dominant digital technology at their disposal. On the other hand, though, the study presents findings that suggest that their practices differ from their American counterparts in significant ways, including the ubiquitous use of smartphones and the strong preference for the Korean KakaoTalk mobile instant messaging (MIM) application to maintain relationships with co-ethnic family and friends both in the U.S. as well as in Korea.

The data analyses of both 31 PEIs and 154 completed surveys with the children of Korean immigrants residing in the U.S. reveal a compelling picture of the types of digital media devices these youths use, the distinct patterns of their social interaction via these devices in the context of their everyday lives, and the role of these devices in helping them maintain their ethnic distinctiveness.

Although individual digital media technologies were separately discussed for the purpose of analysis, it should be noted that each interviewee uses multiple devices on a daily basis, and sometimes even simultaneously. For example, Ivy (17, F, Metro),[1] uses both her desktop computer as well as her smartphone to access Facebook and YouTube, not just to browse but also to upload/download content and update her own profiles. She also frequently uses Google on her various devices to educate herself about her ethnic heritage and study alternative perspectives not found in her American school curriculum, perspectives which became influential factors in her ethnic identity development. Just like Ivy, the other tech-savvy interviewees regularly and simultaneously interact with diverse technologies across multiple platforms in order to understand their worlds and negotiate the multiple facets of their identities. Therefore, the devices they use and how they use them, in addition to the content that they consume, then contribute to their perceptions of themselves and the world around them.

## Digital Media Technology and Everyday Life

As the interviewer began by asking each interviewee, "What role do digital media play in your life," what stood out was how articulate and expressive these youths are. They were able to describe in their own words the many ways that digital media are important to them. In the era of digital media technologies, the interviewees involved in the research consider a smartphone, a laptop, an iPod, and other portable computing devices as social necessities, not luxuries. For example, looking at the photograph she took of her phone, Ye Seul, (17, F, Rural) said, "This is my phone. I got it last August, and I can't live without it. It's not a phone. It's way more than that." (see Figure 3.1)

According to Ye Seul, she personalizes her phone with fancy cases, changes the background screen or the color of her text, and downloads ringtones that she then sets for each of her friends in her contact list. She has also become used to being connected—to her music, videos, and SNSs—via her smartphone. When it comes to smartphones, it was found that several interviewees, just like Ye Seul, embellish their smartphones as frequently as they do their bedroom. As these individuals are physically attached to and emotionally identified with their device, their customization of their smartphones becomes a means of self-expression and a demonstration of their identities (Ling, 2007).

In Taehoon's (15, M, Metro) case, he expressed his feeling of attachment toward his smartphone by saying,

> I don't know why, but when my phone died, I felt seriously lost because it wasn't working. It was only for like 30 minutes, but I felt so helpless. I felt like I would die if it didn't work soon.

Just like Ye Seul's and Taehoon's descriptions, Anna (14, F, City) said, "I even take my phone with me when I go to the bathroom. It's always close by, even when I take a shower. Of course, I also take my phone and tablet with me on family vacations."

As was immediately clear from their comments, all the interviewees in this study affirmed the importance of digital media in their everyday lives. For the majority of the interviewees, it seems that they feel deficient and left-behind when going about their lives without their mobile devices, not only because mobile technologies afford them a whole host of new capabilities, more so than what was ever previously possible, but also because such devices are often their most significant link to their peers. It is evident from the interview responses that digital media technologies, particularly smartphones, are sophisticatedly intertwined into these interviewees' lives.

Another feature of the contemporary proliferation of digital media technologies in children's lives concerns where they actually use these technologies. According to Ye Seul,

> When I come back home from school, the first thing I do is turn on my laptop, grab a snack, and go online. I browse websites about my hobbies, watch video clips, and play games until my mom calls me to dinner. After dinner, I go right back to my computer. (see Figure 3.2)

When the interviewer first met Ye Seul at her house, Ye Seul allowed her to look around her room so that she could have a better understanding of her photos regarding her digital media environment and digital media practices. Upon entering Ye Seul's room, the interviewer noticed that the laptop in her photo is indeed placed on her desk. When asked, "What is it like having your own laptop in your bedroom," Ye Seul replied,

> When I have school assignments or projects to do, it's so convenient to have my laptop in my bedroom so I can work late into the night. Also, I can chat with my friends, check their Facebook profiles, or browse their photos while lying in bed.

But, as shown in Figure 3.1, she made clear that she utilizes her iPhone more than any other digital media device because it is often more readily available and more efficient to use regardless of her location.

Not surprisingly, Ye Seul's specific case mirrors many other interviewees' digital media environment and practices. Based upon others' responses, they own and are indeed using digital media technologies—particularly smartphones—not only behind closed bedroom doors but also while on the move. As the digital media devices available to them become more diverse, it appears that the digital media practices in which they are involved on a daily basis become more independent, private, and personal, implying "markedly different ways of being in the world" (Watkins, 2009, p. 49). This is a point to which we will return later.

Just like interviewees during the PEIs, survey participants in the study often use a variety of digital technologies, listed in Table 3.1 below. One of the obvious trends was the increasing use of smartphones, which eclipsed desktop or laptop computers based on participants' responses. Of the 154 participants, 138 (89.6%) reported that they often use smartphones, while 120 (77.9%) reported that they often use desktop or laptop computers (see Table 3.1). The main driver behind the widespread adoption of smartphones by these participants seems to be the back-to-back introductions of the iPhone in 2007 (Chen, 2011; Goggin, 2009) followed immediately by Android-based smartphones (Goggin, 2012). Smartphones represent the convergence of mobile technology, personal computing, and network connectivity (Madianou, 2014, p. 669), allowing participants to carry a single device anywhere at any time and employ it to complete multiple tasks, including browsing the internet, checking MIM text messages and email, getting on Facebook, and using it as an MP3 player.

Although the survey questions did not explicitly address the locations in which they actually use these technologies, during the PEIs, it became clear that most interviewees own such personal digital devices and have integrated them—particularly smartphones—into their personal lives behind closed bedroom doors and in their public lives while on the move with friends and family. Therefore, in terms of technology access, the majority of the children of Korean immigrants in this study has frequent and unfettered access to smartphones and desktop or laptop computers in their everyday lives. This result strongly suggests that digital technology is not simply present in their lives, but that it is a compelling and perhaps necessary part of their being.

Table 3.1. A Variety of Technologies Used by Participants.

| | Generation Status | | |
|---|---|---|---|
| Devices | 1.5 (%) | 2nd(%) | Total(%) |
| Smartphone | 23 (82.1) | 116 (92.1) | 139 (90.3) |
| Tablet computer/iPad | 7 (28) | 33 (26.2) | 40 (26) |
| Mp3 player/iPod | 7 (28) | 37 (29.4) | 44 (28.6) |
| Desktop or laptop computer | 21 (75) | 100 (79.4) | 121 (78.6) |
| Video game console (e.g., Wii) | 1 (3.6) | 23 (18.2) | 24 (15.6) |

Table 3.2. Internet Usage Frequency on Digital Devices.

| | Internet usage frequency on digital devices (%) | | | | |
|---|---|---|---|---|---|
| | Smartphone | Tablet computer/ iPad | Mp3 player/ iPod | Desktop or laptop computer | Video game console |
| Many times a day | 107 (78.1) | 22 (24.2) | 23 (25.8) | 73 (52.1) | 4 (5.1) |
| Once or twice a day | 12 (8.8) | 12 (13.2) | 12 (13.5) | 30 (21.4) | 1 (1.3) |
| Once every few days | 4 (2.9) | 10 (10.9) | 6 (6.7) | 21 (15) | 6 (7.7) |
| About once a week | 1 (.7) | 5 (5.5) | 3 (3.4) | 7 (5) | 4 (5.1) |
| A couple times a month | 6 (4.4) | 8 (8.8) | 9 (10.1) | 1 (0.7) | 3 (3.9) |
| About once a month or less | 7 (5.1) | 34 (37.4) | 36 (40.5) | 8 (5.7) | 60 (76.9) |
| Total | 137 (100) | 91 (100) | 89 (100) | 140 (100) | 78 (100) |

Being born into an environment where smartphones have become a ubiquitous feature of daily life means that participants view accessing the internet, especially via smartphones, as a given. Regarding their internet usage frequency, 107 participants (78.1%) reported accessing the internet via smartphone many times a day, while 73 participants (52.1%) reported the same but via desktop or laptop computer (see Table 3.2). Comparing results for internet use via smartphones also showed an interesting result: 107 (78.1%) participants reported using a smartphone many times a day, while only 12 (8.8%) participants reported using it once or twice a day. Overall, data from the survey indicated that smartphones outpaced all other technologies as the most frequently accessed internet platform. Indeed, similar to results in recent research on American teens and smartphone use (Rideout, 2016), all the interviewed participants in this study affirmed that being connected to their music, videos, and SNSs via their smartphones is a natural part of their daily lives. Thus, as is evident both from the interviews and survey responses, smartphones are sophisticatedly intertwined into these teens' lives as the most convenient devices with which they frequently and easily stay connected to the world around them and to their peers.

During the PEIs, the more we learned about these teens and their digital media practices, the more complex and fascinating their stories became. There was a strong preference for smartphones among all available digital media devices because, as responses showed, smartphones for this group mean deeper and more intimate interactions beyond the simple ability to make and receive telephone calls. The following interview excerpts illustrate the different ways teens interact with their friends using their smartphones:

> As soon as I got my smartphone, the first thing I did was to add my best friend's phone number on my speed dial. For teenagers like me, who is and who isn't in your speed dial is really important. Not family members, though. I'm talking about other kids at school. I think that someone is our close friend if they're in our contact list, and the people on that list are the ones we talk to most often. (Max, 15, M, City)

> Text messaging is really handy because I can think before replying. If I'm talking on the phone, I have to respond right away and I might say something stupid or there might be an awkward pause. Also, I am able to send or receive text messages anytime from anywhere. I text pretty much every day. I text my friends first, and, if I can't reach them, then I usually call them. (Da Hee, 15, F, Metro)

> I use text messages the most because it's the natural and popular way to communicate within my generation. We don't call much. (Jun Soo, 16, M, Rural)

> For me, texting is so fascinating because I can do all my other stuff while I wait for a response. I usually have about five or six text conversations going on at the same time. (Min Joon, 15, M, Metro)

Their quotes bring out the most interesting aspect of how they have embraced smartphones as innovative communication tools for texting, well beyond a means of making voice calls (Rosen, 2010). Based on their responses, it is because of and through their comfort with texting that these teens engage in everyday communication with their peers. More importantly, texting has not only become a major form of communication among these teens, but it also plays a vital role in how they build and maintain their peer culture (Tutt, 2005).

Given the deeply integrated nature of interviewees' texting using their smartphones, the role of texting in their daily social interaction was further explored:

> I usually text my parents, who are both full-time workers, to let them know where I am and when they need to pick me up after school … Sometimes, my parents text me to let me know that they might be home late … Also, while passing by the grocery store or Walgreens, my parents send me a text asking if we need any groceries or if I need anything for school. (Amy, 13, F, Rural)

> On weekends, my friends and I take turns setting up a party in one of our houses. But, we usually set the date and location very last minute. So, we text back-and-forth with as many friends as possible at the same time to decide when and where to meet. We do this instead of calling because we can send and receive texts even at night without our parents finding out. (Andy, 15, M, City)

The above two quotes are illustrations of very instrumental uses of the smartphone through providing practical information (e.g., pickup time, grocery shopping, party planning), while the next quote demonstrates the communicative aspects of being in touch, for the sake of connectivity, a highly gendered form of smartphone use (Lemish & Cohen, 2005).

> Me and my best friend send text messages to each other and gossip about things we think are interesting or important, such as a boy who was very annoying or funny at school. Maybe it sounds silly to you, but even though our conversations don't really have a point, like talking about homework or something, we have fun together when we text. (Sora, 15, F, Metro)

As to its role in their day-to-day relationships, these teens find texting a simple and fundamental way to chat, discuss events, report status updates, coordinate activities, or exchange quick bits of information. As discussed by interviewees, every smartphone user in the study prefers texting to talking in order to build, maintain, and enhance their social connectivity by sharing their daily life circumstances and experiences. As a result, smartphones, particularly through their text messaging function, have not only added another form of technology-assisted communication, but they also have the potential to both construct space in which social interactions can take place and to sustain intimate social networks with friends or family (Vaidyanathan & Latu, 2007).

Moreover, regardless of generation status, both the first-and-a-half generation and second generation survey participants reported that they use texting (66.2%) more frequently when compared with calling (37.9%) (see

Table 3.3). The result of this survey question is consistent with the results of the PEIs, in which every smartphone user preferred texting to calling in their day-to-day relationships. During the PEIs, convenience was frequently cited as the reason for texting over calling. When asked what they meant by convenience, interviewees defined it as the ability to be unbound from a physical place and have the freedom and means to easily reach whomever they need or want at any time. As the data from this study supports, smartphones, particularly because they free users from the constraints of voice-calling, have not only become a major communication tool for these teens, but they have also provided ever diverse ways for them to interact with their friends in their daily lives.

Table 3.3. Calling vs. Texting.

| | Number of Participants (%) | |
|---|---|---|
| Frequency | Texting | Calling |
| Many times a day | 98 (66.2) | 55 (37.9) |
| Once or twice a day | 30 (20.3) | 62 (42.8) |
| Once every few days | 8 (5.4) | 17 (11.7) |
| About once a week | 2 (1.4) | 3 (2.1) |
| A couple times a month | 4 (2.7) | 6 (4.1) |
| About once a month or less | 6 (4) | 2 (1.4) |
| Total | 148 (100) | 145 (100) |

## Photo-sharing Practice Using Smartphones

Another interesting trend about interviewees' smartphone practices is how their social interactions involve not only text messaging, but also the exchange of various media content, particularly photos. When young people were asked to describe their distinct experiences with their smartphone, taking photographs using their phone and sharing them with others was a frequent digital media practice on which they put a lot of emphasis. Ye Seul (17, F, Rural) provided a good example of this practice in describing how she captures time spent together with friends and then shares her pictures with others afterward. "This is one of my favorite photos," she said while presenting a photo of her friends, "which was taken in a restaurant with friends after celebrating my birthday. They all look like they're having fun," she said (see Figure 3.3), and added:

> With my camera phone, I can take snapshots of the great moments in my life and share them with friends and family. My friends and I often walk around downtown to go shopping, stop by a bookstore to check out new books, drop by Chill to talk, or eat at fast food restaurants. To remember these times, we take lots of photos together using one of our smartphones. Sometimes we pose, but sometimes they're more spontaneous. It helps us remember what we experienced together and reminds us of our group friendship.

She further explained how sharing photos of important events, meaningful places, and close friends and family members with others via her smartphone helps everyone involved to reminisce and talk about the shared moments, thereby strengthening their collective social bonds. From her statements, it is clear that the innovative combination of a smartphone and a camera is an essential and powerful catalyst of socialization for her and her friends.

The photo below is of Sora (15, F, Metro) with a powerful expression on her face as she smiles directly into the camera. According to Sora, she handed her smartphone over to her best friend to take this photo because she wanted a picture of herself with "Cha20 Boba Tea." (see Figure 3.4)

When asked further about the meaning of the photo, she replied,

> This was from when I went to my best friend's birthday party. She is like my sister to me. Sometimes, I'm hesitant to try new things because I'm too nervous. For example, at her party, I wasn't going to try this new drink. But, she encouraged me to try it out, and I ended up liking it very much. This was my first time trying Cha20 Boba, so I shared this happy moment with my other friends using my smartphone.

On the surface, Sora's picture is just herself with Cha20 Boba Tea. However, for Sora, this photo represents a deeper experience of trying new things in the company of her best friend. Generally speaking, then, she uses her smartphone and its built-in camera to both capture and share who she is with her other friends. With the example picture above, she specifically expresses salient aspects of her identity for others to see and interpret. In fact, throughout her interview, she stressed being selective in choosing which pictures to share with her peers that she feels best demonstrate her personality, meaning that her smartphone serves as a tool with which she can perform her identity (Ling, 2007).

Unlike Ye Seul and Sora, who took snapshots of special occasions or precious moments, Eun Ji (15, F, Metro) described how she takes photographs of the more casual and intimate moments of her everyday life and sends them to her friends to establish more frequent connections over the course of each day. Pointing to one of those photos she took, she said,

> This picture shows Frostbites, a popular place near my school where my friends and I hang out a lot. Together, there are five girls in our group. On the day of this photograph, one girl couldn't make it, so I sent her this picture of only four gelatos. Because she wasn't there with us, I used my smartphone to remind her that we missed her, and I got an immediate response from her in a text. It said, "I wish I was there. Thank you for your message." I was very glad that I could let her know that I care about her. (see Figure 3.5)

Apparent in Eun Ji's example is how interviewees capture a good portion of their daily lives as images, which they then share via their smartphones as a kind of currency in their culture of immediate communication with others. Further discussion with Eun Ji revealed that the significance of photo-sharing rests in the constructed opportunities for co-participation in each other's everyday lives, rather than in the revisiting of events in particular ways for the purposes of reminiscing. More specifically, the photos seem to provide contextual cues, or points of orientation that invite comments, simple evaluations, or expressions of approval from recipients in relation to the referents being invoked. Photo-sharing practices therefore enable social interactions around and about photographs to take place over smartphones.

The case of Hye Jin (14, F, City) clearly illustrates the importance of photo-sharing for young people.

> This is a picture of my favorite drink. It's a milk bubble tea from Argo tea. I sent my best friend a birthday message—"Happy Birthday to You"—along with this picture of Argo tea's milk bubble tea, which I would like to buy for her. I texted her, "If you want to try it, it will be my treat the next time we meet. Tell me what you think of this milk bubble tea." And, guess what? Her reply said, "It looks good. Yes, I would love to try it. Thanks!" (see Figure 3.6)

Hye Jin's sending this image to her best friend reveals three important facets of their relationship. First of all, she uses the photo to express to her best friend the kind of drink she enjoys. Second, she solicits her best friend's opinion, which can be interpreted to mean that her best friend's opinion matters to her. Third, through this kind of photo-sharing, they not only connect emotionally, but their relationship also grows in intimacy. The effort to decide on and post appropriate photos, jokes, and comments has become a serious part of her daily activities since everything she posts must appear "cool" in the eyes of an online audience and because her posts will be evaluated as if they are her real life. This case thus suggests that expressions of identity occur simultaneous to the development of social bonding and the enactment of solidarity between them as they share photos. Photo-sharing is therefore a means through which they can build a shared culture and identity.

While examining both their photos and the text under those photos, a variety of American cultural patterns were found. Like those of other American teens, their smartphone screens were full not only of photos and chats about their appearance, but their friends' opinions—both humorous compliments as well as criticism—regularly appear alongside the photos. Their active creation of this photographic world seems to be tightly connected to learning from and updating American culture, which helps them both maintain their American identity and belong to American society in the areas of friendship and behavior (Bae, 2010, p. 94). However, their engagement is of a culturally hybrid nature in that they share content that is also filled with Korean cultural images, gestures, and patterns. Such cultural hybridity in the production of their digital space is an outcome of their complex interplay with their ethnic cultural consumption and reflects their ambivalent cultural positioning (Bae, 2010, p. 99), a point to which we will return later in Chapter 5.

The above set of responses illustrates how photo-sharing via smartphones is now more than ever a normalized form of instant and perpetual communication, allowing users to express their identities in a radically transformative way with their peers (Rivière, 2005, p. 168). Similar to American teens' actively sharing photos via smartphones in their daily lives, interviewees in the study seem to value snapshots far more for their immediate function regarding social bonding and identity formation than simply as mementos. As these teens photograph their world with the frequency, intensity, and expressive capabilities afforded them by smartphones and then share those photos with the groups of which they are a part, it is clear that the camera phone is becoming more than a communication device; it is a visual voice that not only facilitates social interactions but that also helps each individual claim his or her own identity in the context of those interactions (Ling, 2007).

## Adoption of KakaoTalk

In addition to the nearly ubiquitous use of texting and photo-sharing practices among these interviewees, which is common to many diverse youths in westernized countries, a more interesting picture that emerged during the interviews is how they keep in touch with their friends and family overseas using KakaoTalk, a South Korean MIM application available for smartphones, tablets, and computers. Released in March 2010 as South Korea's first MIM

(Choi, 2013; Yoon, 2016a, p. 7), KakaoTalk became the application most used on Korean people's smartphones today owing to its free download. It now has a 98% domestic penetration rate among South Korea's smartphone owners (Choi, 2013; Kim, 2016). Since the introduction of KakaoTalk, email has ceded its position as the communication tool of choice because the former allows for instant communication with anyone using a device on which KakaoTalk is installed.

In particular, KakaoTalk has remade the way Korean Americans communicate with others, bringing profound changes to their lives and those of their family and friends on the other side of the globe. Indeed, as the PEIs showed, a great amount of conversation is taking place using KakaoTalk, the emergence of which has enabled these teens to spend a significant amount of time in MIM with those people who are closest to them (Kim & Lim, 2015). The following screenshot (see Figure 3.7), captured by Rose (17, F, Rural), shows how she frequently uses KakaoTalk on her smartphone to communicate with her friends who are living in Korea.

> I met my friends in the second grade in middle school in Korea, but now I am living in the U.S. It's been several years now. When I wake up here, it's night in Korea. So, it's kind of hard to talk on the phone because of the time difference. That's why I usually chat with them using KakaoTalk. I type mostly in Korean, but sometimes in English. Once I get up, I have about a thousand messages from them. I read them one-by-one and check KakaoTalk several times a day as I wait to hear from them … We may be far apart, but I feel that I am still a part of my friends' lives and they are a part of mine because of KakaoTalk. It's very important for me to know about the details of my friends' daily lives in Korea because I don't want to be a stranger when I visit them in the future.

Rose's example demonstrates that distance does not necessarily diminish the strong connections these youths have with their peers back in Korea. Her friends may not live in the U.S. with her, but her relationships with them continue to grow even after her immigration. She thus maintains solid ties with her friends in Korea through KakaoTalk despite residing in the U.S. For her, KakaoTalk soothes her feelings of homesickness and creates the virtual social interactions that allow her group to feel connected in ways they would otherwise not be able, thereby furnishing her with a sense of belonging. Her interview hints at the complexities of how immigrant children positioned between two cultures engage in different patterns of social interaction, further shaping their ethnic identities while raising compelling questions about how they understand their identities in the U.S. This is a point that will be elaborated on later.

For several interviewees in addition to Rose, KakaoTalk is the most significant lifeline they have to their friends, no matter in which country they may live. In referring to KakaoTalk as a social necessity, Maria (16, F, City) stated,

> I use regular texts with my American or Korean American friends here, but I use KakaoTalk with a couple of Korean friends who are living in Korea because it is free to use as long as I have access to a smartphone, tablet, or computer.

Similarly, Sarah (15, F, Metro) said,

> I mostly use KakaoTalk with the people who don't live around here so that it won't cost money to text. For example, I usually use it with my friends who live in Canada and Korea, and a few of my Korean American friends also have single and group conversations in KakaoTalk going on at the same time.

According to the interviewees, cost is a consideration in maintaining international connections, so communicating over the internet is an attractive alternative to costly texting and calling.

Consistent with other interviewees, John (15, M, Metro) added,

> Most of the people who I use regular text messaging or Facebook chat with live in the U.S. … But, since I also have KakaoTalk on my smartphone, I use it with my family and relatives in Korea. We often exchange emoticons, pictures, videos, and voice clips through KakaoTalk.

As described in the quotes above, from early morning to well into the night, interviewees unceasingly exchange KakaoTalk messages on their smartphones. Many use its group chat function, a feature enabling KakaoTalk users to send a single text message to a group chatroom (Yoon, 2016b, p. 8). Along with one-on-one conversations, they maintain several group chats for the purpose of setting up meetings, engaging in Bible study fellowships, or sharing relevant information about topics including K-pop concerts or daily news from popular Korean websites. Others make use of KakaoTalk's function that lets users browse an album of every photo uploaded to a chatroom. In so doing, each group members can cherish the symbolic meanings associated with shared content. As an atypical example, the memorable messages or interactions within a group chat are saved by capturing screenshots of the chat and then uploading them to the chatroom for everyone to see and remember.

Individual chatroom elements can also be customized in terms of appearance to speak to a group's shared identity, whether that relates to hobbies, culture, or religious activities. The KakaoTalk chatroom thus became an important space in which these interviewees remain actively engaged in ongoing conversations as they perform daily life at home, school, and in social settings.

In chatrooms where KakaoTalk users are actively engaged in group conversations, the size of the groups is quite small, usually encompassing between three to ten members, and the group members are intimately familiar with one another. Although some of the group members were geographically close, others are geographically distant, yet their interactions with interviewees continue because KakaoTalk allows them to keep up with and stay involved in each other's lives despite being so far apart. Furthermore, not only do group members have an emotional attachment to the content that is shared in the chatroom, but they also cherish the virtual space itself, hence their personalizing it by changing the chat title and background, making a group logo, or defining the group chatroom as a place where people far away can visit and be connected. In these intimate settings, they engage in idle chitchat, pass along gossip, and share countless moments of their lives. The conversations themselves are frequently active, are casually conducted in various shortened words and expressions, and are essential for following and commenting on important events in each group member's life. By interacting in this way, the interviewees demonstrate a high degree of understanding about their KakaoTalk contacts, maintaining relationships that might otherwise have faded had they not had the app at their disposal.

Among the users of KakaoTalk in this study, one case in particular stands out. David (17, M, Rural) explains how his life is organized around KakaoTalk in a way that makes it seem as if he still resides in Korea. As such, his smartphone screen is dominated by a steady stream of KakaoTalk messages from family and friends in Korea. The example picture below is drawn from an actual exchange between David and his father, who is currently residing in Korea. (see Figure 3.8)

In the interview, David talked through the context and circumstances of these exchanges and why they had been enacted in particular ways. He began by highlighting what it means for his parents to live so far away from him. He then articulated their ever-present concern for his safety and well-being and how he turned to KakaoTalk as a means to give them status updates about his daily routines or circumstances and allay their concerns. For David, the significance of his intensive engagement with his parents via KakaoTalk, in which they are immersed in the minutiae of his everyday life in the U.S., is that he cultivates their trust, enabling his relationship with them to grow in intimacy. With the help of KakaoTalk, his life at present is therefore still very connected to his parents in Korea, thereby preserving a sense of family engagement despite the substantial distance between them. He also pointed out that through regular conversations via KakaoTalk, his parents came to better appreciate and understand cross-cultural differences, especially between American multiculturalism and Korea's traditionally more homogenous culture (Nedelcu, 2012, p. 12). Because of his coexisting in two different cultures, David sometimes expressed bi-cultural orientations and perspectives towards his social world and ethnic identity, characteristics which were noticed in other interviewees as well and which will be discussed later.

Here, David's case delicately illustrates the far-reaching impact of KakaoTalk on his life as well as that of his parents in Korea. In the past, calling over the telephone, writing a letter, or sending an email was the preferred method of communication with his parents. Since the arrival of KakaoTalk, however, communication with his family has stabilized and greatly increased, both in terms of frequency and the sheer amount of conversations. As smartphones become increasingly integrated into the daily lives of immigrant families, and as they enable them to always be online and connected, they offer Korean immigrant families a sense of simultaneity and coherence (Yoon, 2015). Korean immigrant families also prefer to use KakaoTalk over Facebook because parents can better monitor their children's daily routines through the app (Yoon, 2016b, p. 10). For example, parents who send a KakaoTalk message to their child will then receive a notification alerting them when their child has opened the message. Knowing that their parents have been notified, many children then feel compelled to respond in a timely manner (Yoon, 2016a, p. 9).

Among the various other appeals of KakaoTalk, one key innovation worthy of more discussion is its text messaging feature. Although text messaging these days is a regular feature of most monthly smartphone plans (AT&T, T-Mobile, Verizon, and Sprint offer unlimited calling and text messaging, for example), when smartphones were first introduced, each text message incurred a nominal cost. By contrast, MIM apps such as KakaoTalk have no user fees, run on multiple platforms, have group chat functions, and, unlike SMS, are not tied to particular service providers (Oghuma, Chang, Libaque-Saenz, Park, & Rho, 2015). Especially for immigrant families, the cost of sending international text messages, not to mention the high cost of international phone calls, decimated monthly budgets until apps such as KakaoTalk began to significantly reduce the cost of international communication. As mobile phones evolved into smartphones with increasingly powerful and convenient new features, mobile data plans rapidly came down in price and MIM text messaging outshone SMS by incorporating voice and video call functions, resulting in huge revenue losses for telecoms giants.

In addition to its overall cost-saving nature, KakaoTalk relies on user profiles that include phone numbers and photos, meaning that connecting with others is relatively simple because the application can scan a phone's contact list for other KakaoTalk users and automatically add them to KakaoTalk's contact list (Choi, 2013, p. 65). This scan happens automatically whenever a user adds a new phone number to his or her phone's contact list.

The same is true for others as well, however, so any KakaoTalk user with your phone number can see your KakaoTalk profile. This accessibility has translated into profiles playing a critical role in introducing users and serving as the hubs of interaction, thereby encouraging users to consciously construct their profiles to be seen by others. Once a profile photo is uploaded to the KakaoTalk network, it can be viewed by multiple users in the same network, creating greater possibilities for recapturing old ties as well as new communicative opportunities that would most likely not exist offline (Kim, 2016).

Although the original purpose of the KakaoTalk profile was to inform others of the user's identity, users have come to construct them as public diaries, revealing private visual information regarding tastes and lifestyles and thereby contributing to the overall public discourse. KakaoTalk allows users to send and receive a mixture of texts, videos, and digital gifts, but it is with photos that users can compose their life stories. For example, one of the interviewees arranged his profile photo album as a representation of his identity and memory, so that swiping from photo to photo has become a way for him to take stock of his life and its trajectory. Indeed, KakaoTalk users check their profiles as often as they upload photos, a self-reflective practice stemming from their awareness that visitors viewing their profile regularly leave feedback messages (Kim, 2016). For this reason, some of the interviewees were concerned that their friends might disapprove of their profile photos. By asking their close friends prior to uploading whether the photos they choose are appropriate for their profile, they can mitigate any negative feedback they might receive that could compel them to instantly change or delete the offensive photos. Based on this behavior, interviewees have created a distinct culture of expression in their careful selecting, posting, and organizing of profile photos on KakaoTalk.

One of the most commonly cited reasons behind the widespread adoption and use of KakaoTalk among this group was that the app provides delivery notification and a timestamp for messages. Every user can see the exact time at which messages were sent, and the app displays a number next to each message in the chatroom indicating how many have yet to read it, an indication which disappears once everyone in the chatroom has seen the message. Users can further control delivery notifications for chatrooms both individually and as a whole (Kim & Lim, 2015). As discussed previously in David's case, many of the interviewees' parents are using KakaoTalk to monitor their children at school, arrange their pick-up time and location after school, and maintain intimacy with their children throughout the day, tasks which are greatly aided by the application's messaging confirmation features. As KakaoTalk makes parents feel more at ease, this in turn has led interviewees to not just download KakaoTalk on their own smartphones, but to stay closely attached to it throughout each day.

In order to stay competitive against the juggernaut that is Facebook, Kakao Corporation further developed KakaoStory, a separate social networking app that links to a user's KakaoTalk account and allows him or her to post pictures, animated GIFs, and emoticons to create stories (Choi, 2013, p. 67). Korean immigrants in Canada, for example, frequently used KakaoStory to narrate their lives by uploading photos, postings that became more than idle musings about the day and instead served as essential components of daily life for these immigrants (Yoon, 2016b, p. 8). Just as Yoon (2016b) found with Korean immigrants in Canada, interviewees in this study are also using KakaoStory to network with their local co-ethnic friends as well as to communicate with family members or friends in Korea. In sum, the rapid adoption of KakaoTalk and its related applications has been fueled by the need for its users to stay connected to their family and friends, and adapting to its many uses has become a widely accepted cultural norm among Korean and Korean American users (Choi, 2013).

The richness of interviewees' responses leaves little doubt that their frequent use of KakaoTalk on their smartphones bolsters the intensity and intimacy of their relationships with their family and Korean friends. As it furthers global connections through a compression of time and space, KakaoTalk thus appears to provide these interviewees with an important platform on which to develop or enhance the friendships and relationships that are instrumental to their ethnic identity formation. Through this kind of virtual socialization, these teens not only connect on a daily and intimate basis with their socio-cultural context of origin, but they may also learn ways of grasping and exploring their ethnic background and cultural lifestyles, thereby influencing their ethnic identities (boyd & Ellison, 2007; McPhail, 2006).

Furthermore, survey responses summarized in Table 3.4 below provide additional strong evidence to support the significant finding from the PEIs that these children of Korean immigrants in the U.S. frequently use KakaoTalk, which is rarely discussed in research literature. These results indicate that participants in the study most often use Facebook and KakaoTalk as their regular text messaging applications in their daily social interactions.

Most of the participants, regardless of generation status, use Facebook as their most frequent text messaging application in their daily social interactions; the vast majority of both first-and-a-half generation and second generation participants reported using Facebook for text messaging (see Table 3.4). Two thirds of the users also said they use it many times a day.

The next most frequent text messaging application was KakaoTalk, which was cited by over three-quarters of the participants as their text messaging application. Although KakaoTalk ranked behind Facebook as the second most frequently used text messaging application for both first-and-a-half and second generation participants, it is worth noting that a majority of both groups still use KakaoTalk very often for their daily social interactions in the U.S. This is perhaps not surprising when considering it is a South Korean instant messenger application available for smartphones, tablets, and computers, but its lack of popularity among mainstream Americans suggests that its popularity in this study has important cultural significance. It is important to note, though, that the first-and-a-half generation participants have a stronger preference for it and use it more frequently than their second generation counterparts. One explanation for this difference might be that the former spent at least some of their formative years in Korea, during which they made close personal friends with whom they want or feel the need to keep in touch with after relocating to the U.S. Among those who use KakaoTalk as reported during the PEIs, Rose's and David's cases in particular stand out: both first-and-a-half generation interviewees explained how their lives are organized around KakaoTalk in a way that makes it seem as if they still reside in Korea. As such, their smartphone screens are dominated by a steady stream of KakaoTalk messages from family and friends in Korea. Even though their daily activities and social interactions take place primarily with their American friends in America, their engagement with KakaoTalk seems to counteract geographical distance as it both foregrounds and strengthens bonds with family members or friends who are living in Korea.

However, because of their coexisting in two different cultures, even several second generation interviewees confirmed their engagement with KakaoTalk in order to keep in touch with their local co-ethnic friends or their friends and family overseas. In fact, the depth of their responses shows precisely how their prolific engagement with KakaoTalk for the purposes of networking and communication solidifies relationships they have with family and co-ethnic friends both in America and Korea. Such smartphone-enabled online interactions are a key factor in how these youths both form and solidify important friend and family connections in the process of developing their own ethnic identity.

Table 3.4. KakaoTalk.

| | Generation Status | | | | | |
|---|---|---|---|---|---|---|
| | 1.5 | | | 2nd | | |
| | Text messaging applications | | | | | |
| Frequency | KakaoTalk | Facebook | Skype | KakaoTalk | Facebook | Skype |
| Many times a day | 20 (83.3) | 18 (66.7) | 3 (17.6) | 47 (49.5) | 75 (66.4) | 9 (13) |
| Once or twice a day | 2 (8.3) | 5 (18.5) | 1 (5.9) | 18 (18.9) | 18 (15.9) | 10 (14.5) |
| Once every few days | 0 | 2 (7.4) | 2 (11.8) | 10 (10.5) | 4 (3.5) | 8 (11.6) |
| About once a week | 0 | 1 (3.7) | 3 (17.6) | 0 | 2 (1.7) | 2 (2.9) |
| A couple times a month | 1 (4.2) | 0 | 3 (17.6) | 4 (4.2) | 7 (6.2) | 9 (13) |
| About once a month or less | 1 (4.2) | 1 (3.7) | 5 (29.4) | 16 (16.8) | 7 (6.2) | 31 (45) |
| Total | 24 (100) | 27 (100) | 17 (100) | 95 (100) | 113 (100) | 69 (100) |

Although the first-and-a-half generation participants are the heaviest users of KakaoTalk, the second generation participants' responses were unexpected. As evidenced by PEI results, which show that most smartphone users among the second generation interviewees have KakaoTalk installed on their smartphones, what the survey results in Table 3.4 seem to suggest is that adoption and use of KakaoTalk even among the second generation participants are considerable. This discovery of KakaoTalk's importance for these children of Korean immigrants in the U.S., both first-and-a-half and second generations, helps fill in gaps in the sparse literature on KakaoTalk adoption among Korean immigrants around the world. As illustrated in the interviewees' responses, we can speculate that participants are expressing their ownership of and attachment to relationships maintained through KakaoTalk. Because KakaoTalk combines the characteristics of MIM and social networking, exploring further how it is used by these children of Korean immigrants to share everyday experiences can provide insight into how they are negotiating their ethnic identities and culturally diversifying their social networks beyond local interactions, the latter of which will be discussed in Chapter 5.

To summarize, the teens who participated in this study have been able to maintain strong ties with their home country through regular contact with family members and friends in far-flung places by using KakaoTalk. Not only has it increased the quantity of communication, but also the quality in that it provides a sense of physical closeness no matter the distance (Benitez, 2012, p. 1446; Wilding, 2006) by facilitating myriad interactions that do not require being physically present, such as sharing customized images that represent one's personality and lifestyle. While KakaoTalk is not dominant in the American mainstream market, the findings here of its centrality in these teens' everyday lives add more cultural significance to the existing body of research by discussing how such ethnically defined cultural behavior—the persistent use of KakaoTalk—is shaping their orientation toward the home country and their ethnic identities by helping them experience more intense emotional attachment to and feelings of simultaneity with their home country.

## Note

1. Identity of interviewees includes a pseudonym, age, F for female and M for Male, and one of three types of areas of residency: Rural for a rural Midwest university town, City for a large Midwestern city, and Metro for a West Coast Metropolitan.

## References

Bae, M. S. (2010). Go Cyworld! Korean diasporic girls producing new Korean femininity. In S. R. Mazzarella (Ed.), *Girl Wide Web 2.0: Revisiting girls, the Internet, and the negotiation of identity* (pp. 91–116). New York, NY: Peter Lang.

Benitez, J. L. (2012). Salvadoran transnational families: ICT and communication practices in the network society. *Journal of Ethnic and Migration Studies*, *38*(9), 1439–1449.

boyd, d. m., & Ellison, N. B. (2007). Social network sites: Definition, history, and scholarship. *Journal of Computer-Mediated Communication*, *13*, 210–230.

Chen, B. (2011). *Always on: How the iPhone unlocked the anything-anytime-anywhere future- and locked us in*. Cambridge, MA: Da Capo Press.

Choi, E. (2013). KakaoTalk, a mobile social platform pioneer. *SERI Quarterly*, 63–70.

Goggin, G. (2009). Adapting the mobile phone: The iPhone and its consumption. *Continuum: Journal of Media and Cultural Studies*, *23*(2), 231–244.

Goggin, G. (2012). Google phone rising: The android and the politics of open source. *Continuum: Journal of Media and Cultural Studies*, *26*(5), 741–752.

Kim, J. (2016). *Branding Korea or marketing ethnicity? Manhattan's Koreatown as a transclave in the global economy*. PhD diss. CUNY Academic Works. Retrieved from http://academicworks.cuny.edu/gc_etds/1268

Kim, D.-j., & Lim, Y.-k. (2015). Dwelling places in KakaoTalk: Understanding the roles and meanings of chatrooms in mobile instant messengers. In *Proceedings of the 18th ACM Conference on Computer Supported Cooperative Work & Social Computing*, (CSCW'15), 775–784. ACM, New York, NY, USA. doi: http://dx.doi.org/10.1145/2675133.2675198

Lemish, D., & Cohen, A. (2005). On the gendered nature of mobile phone culture in Israel. *Sex Roles, 52*(7–8), 511–525.

Ling, R. (2007). Children, youth, and mobile communication. *Journal of Children and Media, 1*(1), 60–67.

Madianou, M. (2014). Smartphones as Polymedia. *Journal of Computer-Mediated Communication, 19*, 667–680.

McPhail, T. (2006). *Global communication: Theories, stakeholders and trends*. (2nd ed.). Malden, MA: Wiley-Blackwell.

Nedelcu, M. (2012). Migrants' new transnational habitus: Rethinking, migration through a cosmopolitan lens in the digital age. *Journal of Ethnic and Migration Studies, 38*(9), 1339–1356.

Oghuma, A., Chang, Y., Libaque-Saenz, C., Park, M.-C., & Rho, J. J. (2015). Benefit-confirmation model for post-adoption behavior of mobile instant messaging application: A comparative analysis of KakaoTalk and Joyn in Korea. *Telecommunications Policy, 39*(8), 658–677.

Rideout, V. (2016). Measuring time spent with media: The common sense census of media use by US 8- to 18-year-olds. *Journal of Children and Media, 10*(1), 138–144. doi: 10.1080/17482798.2016.1129808

Rivière, C. (2005). Mobile camera phones: A new form of "being together" in daily interpersonal communication. In R. Ling & P. E. Pedersen (Eds.), *Mobile communications: Re-negotiation of the social sphere* (pp. 167–185). London, UK: Springer.

Rosen, L. D. (2010). *Rewired: Understanding the igeneration and the way they learn*. New York, NY: Palgrave Macmillan.

Tutt, D. (2005). Mobile performances of a teenager: A study of situated mobile phone activity in the living room. *Convergence, 11*(2), 58–75.

Vaidyanathan, L., & Latu, S. (2007). Social consequences of cellular (cell) phones. *Proceedings from 18th Australasian Conference on Information Systems (ACIS) 2007.*

Watkins, S. C. (2009). *The young and the digital: What the migration to social-network sites, games, and anytime, anywhere media means for our future*. Boston, MA: Beacon Press.

Wilding R. (2006). Virtual intimacies? Families communicating across transnational contexts. *Global Networks*, 6(2), 125–142.

Yoon, W. K. (2015). *Global pulls on the Korean communities in Sao Paulo and Buenos Aires*. Lanham, MD: Lexington Books.

Yoon, K. (2016a). The cultural appropriation of smartphones in Korean Transnational families. In S. S. Lim (Ed.), *Mobile communication and the family: Asian experiences in technology domestication* (pp. 93–108). New York, NY: Springer.

Yoon, K. (2016b). Korean migrants' use of the Internet in Canada. *Journal of International Migration and Integration, 18*(2), 547–562.

Figure 3.1. My Smartphone.
Source: Photo by Ye Seul.

Figure 3.2. My Laptop.
Source: Photo by Ye Seul.

Figure 3.3. Chilling With Friends.
Source: Photo by Ye Seul.

Figure 3.4. Boba Tea for the First Time.
Source: Photo by Sora.

Figure 3.5. Frostbites.
Source: Photo by Eun Ji.

Figure 3.6. My Favorite Bubble Tea.
Source: Photo by Hye Jin.

Figure 3.7. KakaoTalking With Friend Group in Korea.
Source: Photo by Rose.

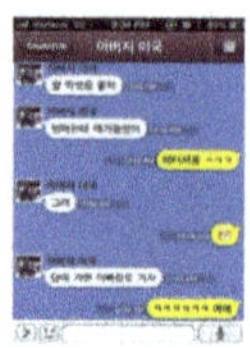

Figure 3.8. KakaoTalking With My Father.
Source: Photo by David.

· 4 ·

# DIGITAL MEDIA AND THE CONSTRUCTION OF KOREAN IDENTITY

Our second research question of this study was: How do these youths engage in the exploration and the development of their ethnic identity? We discovered in this study evidence on the Korean ethnic identity of the participants, demonstrating that contrary to expectations, first-and-a-half and second generation immigrant youths do not differ from each other in either the centrality of their ethnic identity or most of their digital media practices in their everyday lives. Both groups are actively engaged in using digital media to negotiate their culture of origin and their place in the world in which they are growing up. Comparing the results of this study with studies on immigration and identity construction prior to the advent of digital media suggest that the latter greatly facilitate the ability to maintain a strong ethnic identity, thereby shaping a different immigration experience.

## Measuring Ethnic Identity

Six questions in the MEIM–R (Multigroup Ethnic Identity Measure-Revised, see Chapter One) part of the survey questionnaire, asked participants to use a Likert scale to rank a variety of statements regarding the ways in which they have explored and committed to their ethnic group. The list of six close-ended items of the MEIM–R, which assess exploration of and commitment to one's ethnic identity, is shown in the Appendix B. The items in the exploration factor were concerned with learning more about one's ethnic group as well as their participation in ethnic cultural practices. They include the following three statements: "I have spent time trying to find out more about my own ethnic group, such as its history, traditions, customs, and pop cultures"; "I have often done things that will help me understand my ethnic background better"; and "I have often talked to other people in order to learn more about my ethnic group." The commitment factor assessed whether participants had a positive affirmation of his or her group, based on social identity theory (Tajfel & Turner, 1986), and a clear sense of commitment as defined by Marcia (1980). The three statements that explored the commitment to one's ethnic identity were: "I have a strong sense of belonging to my own ethnic group"; "I understand pretty well what my ethnic group membership means to me"; and "I feel a strong attachment towards my own ethnic group."

Using the MEIM–R instrument's cumulative scale, which measures ethnic identity on a scale of 1–5 (with 1 being "strongly disagree" and 5 being "strongly agree"), the sample mean of the total 154 participants was 3.83 ($SD$ = .89). Most of the means of the individual questions were close to 4, which is an indication of a strong (although not the strongest) ethnic identity (Phinney & Ong, 2007). The MEIM–R can also be analyzed according to the two subscales: the mean of exploration questions (3.61) reflects the overall strength of ethnic identity exploration, and the mean of the commitment questions (4.05) assesses the overall strength of commitment. The sample means for both subscales therefore indicate that participants are strongly engaged in both exploration and commitment, suggesting that the results of this survey data mirror a phenomenon frequently reported among the interviewees during the PEIs.

To better understand in detail what separates first-and-a-half and second generation participants in terms of their ethnic identity exploration and commitment, we compared the MEIM–R data for each group using the MEIM–R instrument's cumulative scale, the sample mean of all 28 first-and-a-half generation participants was 3.99, while the exploration mean was 3.69 and the commitment mean was 4.29. Thus, the sample means for the subscales indicate that first-and-a-half generation participants are strongly engaged in both exploration and commitment.

Using the MEIM–R instrument's cumulative scale, the sample mean of the total 126 second generation participants was 3.80, while the exploration mean was 3.60 and the commitment mean was 4.00. Thus, the sample means for the subscales indicate that second generation participants are also strongly engaged in both exploration and commitment.

While the exploration mean for the first-and-a-half generation group was 3.69, the exploration mean for the second generation group was nearly identical at 3.60. As discussed earlier in the literature review, one fundamental difference that researchers highlight between first-and-a-half and second generation groups is that second generation youth differ in that their exposure to American culture begins from birth, which means they grow up as Americans with no compelling need to learn about their parents' culture (Bandon, 1994; Lehrer, 1996). However, the results of this survey data are not congruent with past literature. As contrasting evidence, the particular case of second generation participants in this study shows that they do in fact make as much of an effort as first-and-a-half generation youths to not only learn more about their parents' culture, but to also explore their own ethnic identity.

While the commitment mean for the first-and-a-half generation group was 4.29, which indicates a very strong commitment to their ethnic identity, the commitment mean for the second generation group was 4.00, suggesting that they too feel strongly about and are committed to their ethnic identity. As discussed earlier in the literature review, another difference between the two groups of interviewees is that those in the first-and-a-half generation group spent at least some of their formative years in Korea, meaning that they were born into their native language and culture and brought with them to America a more diverse blend of linguistic, cultural, and social beliefs and practices (Bandon, 1994; Lehrer, 1996). So, compared to those in the second generation, first-and-a-half generation participants would be expected to have a stronger sense of belonging to their ethnic group or desire to restore their connection with their ethnic identity that has somewhat eroded since their immigration. However, survey responses showed that, just like their counterparts, second generation participants possess a strong attachment to their original culture and ethnic group, which is surprising considering they were instead born into American culture. Thus, the results of the survey data are not consistent with those reported in past studies that suggested that American-born descendants of immigrants are less in touch with their ethnic identities than those born in their parents' home country (Gans, 2004).

The last question on the MEIM–R asked participants to identify their "ethnic group." When participants responded to this question, they provided a wide variety of responses. For the purposes of analysis, their responses were classified into six categories, further described below.

Respondents' self-reported ethnicity was used to classify participants into six major ethnic descriptions (see Table 4.1). Just over one third of the participants stated their country-of-origin identity as South Korean or Korean while 41.0% claimed themselves as Korean American, with very few participants identifying solely as American. Clearly, the most commonly reported ethnic group among the participants was Korean American (41.0%), showing consistency with the results of the PEIs, in which 30 of 31 interviewees identified themselves as Korean American. Similar to Park's (2009) study that argued that the acculturation processes of second generation immigrants are in fact acculturation to the "Korean American" ethnic group and de-acculturation from "Americans," the findings of this study confirmed a similar phenomenon, a tendency known in her research as "re-acculturation," which is becoming acculturated back into the originating ethnic group since it means going back to being "Korean American" from "American" among young Korean Americans (p. 80).

The second most common response for country-of-origin identity was South Korean or Korean (36.8%) among both first-and-a-half and second generation groups. Interestingly, among second generation participants, 34.5% adopted country-of-origin identity as either South Korean or Korean, a result that is not consistent with previous research. Although the literature indicates that children born in the U.S. to immigrant parents are more likely to define themselves as Americans (Min, 2002; Min & Kim, 2000; Thai, 2002), a little more than one third of the second generation participants in this study adopted the ethnic identity of their parents. Despite the Americanization that they already undergo, they seem to choose their ethnic identities over a purely American identity due to several factors that exert a turn away from American-made labels, such as their parents' role in their bilingualism, summer cultural and language school in Korea or in a local church, and, more importantly, the instant connectivity with Korea that is enabled by digital media devices.

In sum, it is important to understand the key factors and means associated with ethnic identity formation and reconstruction of the contemporary second generation because their identities are not always stable (Song, 2003). The existing research on ethnic identification using segmented assimilation theory has emphasized several factors including parental background (e.g., parental education), family arrangement (e.g., nuclear family versus multigenerational living arrangement), and modes of incorporation (e.g., ethnic community) (Portes & Zhou, 1993), all of which act as reinforcing agents for ethnic identity. Our research, however, found that digital media technology as a site for exploration of and commitment to ethnic identity adds yet another dimension to the assimilation process as it relates to ethnic identification, a process that is becoming more dynamic and complex as virtual spaces confound these youths' lived reality.

Table 4.1. The Most Commonly Reported Ethnic Groups.

| | Generation Status | | |
|---|---|---|---|
| Reported Ethnic Groups | 1.5 (%) | 2nd (%) | Total (%) |
| South Korean | 1 (3.6) | 1 (.9) | 2 (1.39) |
| Korean | 12 (42.9) | 39 (33.6) | 51 (35.42) |
| Korean American | 10 (35.7) | 49 (42.2) | 59 (40.97) |
| Asian | 2 (7.1) | 6 (5.2) | 8 (5.56) |
| Asian American | 3 (10.7) | 19 (16.4) | 22 (15.28) |
| American | 0 | 2 (1.7) | 2 (1.39) |
| Total | 28 (100) | 116 (100) | 144 (100) |

## SNSs as Platforms for Socialization and Identity Performance

A central topic introduced by interviewees was how accessing SNSs via smartphone is becoming a more ubiquitous form of socialization. In one study, 50% of Facebook users reported accessing the site via their smartphones (Mansumitrchai, Park, & Chiu, 2012, p. 142). For example, Hye Jin (14, F, City) used her photographs below to talk about frequently accessing her SNSs via smartphone to design and update her Facebook page. She said,

> Social networks are easy to access on smartphones, so I regularly use Instagram, a photo-sharing app, because of my friends. They all have the app on their phones, and they all use it a lot, so it's fun to see what they post. (see Figure 4.1) I stay up late almost every night working on my Facebook page in my room to decide what to share. I love letting my friends know what is going on with me, uploading my favorite photos, adding my feelings about those photos, and talking about my taste in music or movies.

Hye Jin's explanation of her own SNS use also captures the daily experiences of many other interviewees. For them as well, participating in SNSs has become constitutive of the particular ways in which they interact socially in order to connect with others, increase their common bonds, and strengthen a sense of belonging (boyd, 2007).

In the context of "hanging out," Hye Jin spends hours each night elaborately constructing her own Facebook profile, surfing from one friend's profile to another's, writing personal messages on their profiles, and extensively commenting back-and-forth with her friends—all forms of conversation that collectively result in socialization. She was very proud to share that she has about 600 friends on Facebook and 200 followers on Instagram, seeming to consider more online friends as a sign of her popularity. Her routine of decorating and checking her profile comes from her awareness that she is being evaluated by others. According to Illouz's (2007) study about online self-identity expression, showcasing a profile online for all to see changes the private self into a public performance since it represents the user and serves as the hub from which all subsequent interactions stem. Hye Jin demonstrates a deliberate effort to upload photos appropriate to her circumstance, specifically regarding the need to appear cool in the eyes of an online audience. As she expressed her attachment to her Facebook page, it became clear both how much she cherishes it and how much she enjoys personalizing the virtual space, much as we do our own homes.

For example, Hye Jin often changes her main page's title and background so as to reflect her particular tastes and identity, expressing ownership of her online self through a high degree of personalization that takes a great deal more effort and time. Her description of how she constructs her Facebook profile not only mirrors that of other second generation interviewees, but is also similar to the process by which interviewees create KakaoTalk profiles, as discussed in the previous chapter. However, while updating profiles on KakaoTalk via smartphone is more popular among first-and-a-half generation interviewees because they have more friends overseas in Korea, where KakaoTalk is ubiquitous in daily life, modifying profiles on SNSs via smartphone is more common among second generation interviewees because they have more friends locally in the U.S., where Facebook is instead most people's daily driver for social networking.

When asked, "How does Facebook influence your relationships with those friends," after pausing for a few seconds, she answered,

> Facebook is an important part of my life. If you don't connect with your friends on Facebook, then you are missing a huge part of their lives, and if you are missing a huge part of their lives, then it's really hard to be friends with them.

Hye Jin's simple quote makes clear the role of SNSs in her social life as enablers of the very socialization that strengthens her relationships with her friends.

Interestingly, she further discussed how two different pictures that she had posted represent her views of American and Korean cultures, with a focus on specific cultural customs that, respectively, converge with and diverge from her American friends.

> My favorite American holiday is Christmas because my family decorates our Christmas tree and wraps presents together, and we start putting the presents under the tree as we get closer to Christmas. This is a picture of the area where I live on a White Christmas day.

Her enthusiasm in describing Christmas as her favorite American holiday and the importance of what she does together with her family on that day seem very apparent, reflecting a certain level of comfort in showing her appreciation for Western cultural customs. (see Figure 4.2)

The second picture, however, spoke to her favorite Korean traditional holiday.

> My favorite Korean holiday is *Suhl-Nahl* [Korean New Year's Day] because family and relatives give cash as a kind of blessing to children and grandchildren on this day. This is the money I got from my grandparents. It's a common cultural tradition in Korean families, and I usually post pictures of it on Facebook to remember it. (see Figure 4.3)

She emphasized that celebrating *Suhl-Nahl* and following Korean cultural customs allowed her and her family to keep their Korean ethnicity even while living in the U.S. Moreover, in posting the *Suhl-Nahl* picture in particular, she saw it as an opportunity to share her culture of origin with peers outside of her ethnic community. As Lee's (2003) research would suggest, Hye Jin seems to exercise her ethnic identity by actively keeping and participating in Korean cultural activities, such as celebrating traditional holidays with her family. Her posting photos of those traditional holidays on Facebook, then, is more than just a simple celebration; it demonstrates her desire to make herself and her cultural traditions visible in such a way that she appears distinct from her non-Korean friends.

Hye Jin frequently posts profile pictures, background pictures, and status messages that reflect some aspect of Korean culture and, more importantly, its centrality in her life. However, her active creation of this online bi-cultural world does not imply subordination to either American or Korean culture, but rather it is her reenacting both cultures with the inclusion of her own unique voice (Bae, 2010, p. 94). Such bi-cultural behavior with regards to sharing photographs on SNSs formed a noticeable subculture among the interviewees in this study, seeming to help them connect with and express their ethnicity (Panagakos, 2003, p. 202).

In her interview, Jackie (15, F, City) explained how she pulled some of her pictures from Facebook and spliced them together, showing her and her friends in pre-adolescence in the top half and as teenagers in the bottom half, in order to visualize her experience of growing up in two different social and cultural worlds. In explaining her motivation, she addressed some concerns that might have gone into how she selected her photos, concerns that tease out interesting facets of her identity. She said,

> I believe that your Facebook page says a lot about who you were in the past … who you are in the present … So, these pictures show my past and present …, and maybe even who I might be in the future … (see Figure 4.4)

Reflecting on her bi-cultural social circle, Jackie said,

> Because I have more than one culture in me, I have friends from different cultures. The white girl in the picture was one of the first Americans I met and felt comfortable hanging out with. She was really sweet and cool when I met her, and she is still that way today. The other two girls in the picture are my Korean friends. I grew up playing with all of them during my childhood, and I still keep in touch with them by sharing pictures and talking about funny events or people at school so that we can know what's going on in each other's lives.

Based on her photos and her detailed explanations, her relationships with her Korean and American friends are as meaningful and strong now as when she was a child, and the element of time progression in the combined photo seems to indicate her desire to maintain those friendships and the cultural links they represent even into the future.

Jackie also reported, in terms of online socialization,

> I have accounts on a few popular sites, such as Facebook and YouTube. I log in several times a day to see my friends' photos and posts and to read their comments on my photos. I spend more time on those sites especially when I become interested in talking about a certain topic or hobby.

For her, SNSs are like a virtual smorgasbord where she can come to know many things about her friends, about whom she clearly cares, and invest herself deeply in their lives. In terms of socializing outside of SNSs, unlike other interviewees who prefer socializing separately with their Korean and American friends because of their comfort with only speaking either Korean or

English, she seems to prefer socializing with a single group of friends from different cultures. Her comfort with mingling simultaneously with her white American friends and those friends who share her Korean ancestry shows her openness and flexibility in developing a dual frame of reference.

Annie (14, F, Rural) described the initial culture shock she felt on her first day of school in America before then detailing a positive SNS experience, which introduced her to her first local co-ethnic friend and lessened the anxiety she was feeling. She said,

> When I first arrived in the U.S., I experienced culture shock. I was very shy because I wasn't very good at English. So, my interactions with other kids at school were very limited … While I was struggling to learn this new culture, Sophia was the one who helped me through it all. (see Figure 4.5)

In describing the relationship she developed with Sophia, her first local co-ethnic friend, Annie said,

> By looking through my friends' lists of Facebook friends, I could still see some of their information even though they were not my Facebook friends. That's how I was able to find and connect with Sophia, who is now my best friend. Because I didn't know a lot about American culture or American people …, she gave me a better idea of how American people think and talk, and this helped me adjust to the new culture.

SNSs became a very powerful means by which Annie could locate and reach out to American-born co-ethnic friends who might be able to ease her into American life and simultaneously provide her with emotional support. According to Annie,

> Compared to other non-Korean friends, Sophia didn't mind my broken English … I also didn't mind her broken Korean. Yet, I learned so much about this new culture from her explanations about American life. So, she was like my teacher. She introduced me to so many new things … It's funny, but I then became like her Korean teacher … For example, I became a fan of Justin Bieber and his song "Baby," while she became a fan of Psy and his hit song "*Gangnam Style*."

Based on her discussion, forming and maintaining her relationship with Sophia by Facebook proved beneficial to both girls. On one hand, it assisted Annie's integration into her host culture (Chen, 2009). On the other hand, it appeared to expose Sophia to more about her own ethnic heritage. In this context, Facebook enhanced not just the building of social networks more generally or the development of co-ethnic friendships more specifically, but it facilitated the sharing of critical information about each other's cultural needs. Such interactions, centered on the mutual exchange of information, exist elsewhere on the internet as well in a number of Korean websites and applications. MissyUSA.com, a popular website for Korean immigrants seeking American cultural information, provides Korean-language news reports about current events in America as a means to help immigrants adjust to the host society (Lee & Katz, 2015; Oh, 2016a). Also, HeyKorean.com, a Korean online community, and online interactions through KakaoTalk help create a sense of connection to and involvement with the larger Korean immigrant community (Lee & Katz, 2015, pp. 615–616; Oh, 2016a & b).

While both Annie and Sophia rely on each other as cultural resources about Korea and America, respectively, it is SNSs, and particularly Facebook, that both link them and facilitate their socialization. Annie's case therefore demonstrates the creativity and flexibility with which these interviewees leverage their SNSs as platforms for locating, connecting with, and socializing with co-ethnic peers, which not only eases their own integration into American culture, but it creates a bi-directional, mutually beneficial relationship of cultural exchange in that each person fulfills the other's cultural interests.

Pointing to a picture of Korean candies as a representation of his attachment to Korean culture, Jimmy (15, M, Metro) described the nostalgic feelings this photo brought up in him about his grandparents, who visited his family in the U.S. a few years ago. He said,

> My grandparents sent me a package all the way from Korea, and it was full of all this Korean candy. They sent me so many bags of Korean candies so that I could share them with my school friends. When I uploaded this picture to Facebook with a note, "Who wants to have these Korean candies?" … Wow, my friends were really excited to try them. (see Figure 4.6)

When asked further about the meaning of this photo, he explained that he was always explicit about his love for American food, but that he used to be ambiguous when it came to Korean food. He reported that he started to eat more Korean food only when his grandparents visited. Prior to that, his intention was to prove to them that choosing to adopt only certain aspects of Korean culture (not eating Korean food, for example) does not make him any less their grandson. As he stated,

> I was clumsy with chopsticks and I didn't like kimchi [spicy, fermented cabbage and one of the most traditional Korean side dishes]. So, they were always like, "You need to care more about your parents' culture ..." So, I tried the Korean candy they brought with them …, and I liked it very much. A few weeks ago, they sent a package full of

> these Korean candies because they remembered how much I enjoyed them ... Every time I look at this picture, it reminds me of my grandparents, who were so sweet to me.

Jimmy's response clearly shows his longing for the time he spent with his grandparents while they were in the U.S., ultimately indicating his intention to maintain ties with them because they represent both Korean culture at large as well as his own personal family heritage. Jimmy continued,

> Meeting my grandparents for the first time as a teenager was awesome for me. During their stay, I ate Korean food and heard the Korean language all the time. Although I couldn't understand everything they said, I felt their love for me ... And, after learning new things about Korean culture, I became much more interested in Korean things.

Since their trip to the U.S., Korean culture has become compelling for Jimmy in such a way that he can relate to it more personally and that encourages him to explore it further. Unlike American mainstream teenagers, in some respects, he seems to use SNSs as a means of expressing his personal experiences that are associated with his ethnic heritage—his "Koreanness"—and the emotional attachment he now has to his grandparents and the culture that they represent.

What is apparent from the interviews is that, for a portion of interviewees, a noticeable mixture of Korean and American cultural elements forms a significant part of their SNS use, their SNSs having been transformed into influential sites of socialization where teens share their personal experiences and produce their own hybrid cultural space. Their routine use of SNSs provides both a channel through which they can make known their personal tastes and ethnic identities (boyd, 2007) and, more significantly, an opportunity to simultaneously reflect on those identities as they are in the process of constructing them (Rosen, 2010). These teens, then, use SNSs not merely as a technological means to connect with others on a surface level, but as a virtual playground in which they continuously shape and reshape their ethnic identities while establishing their positions regarding the cultures of which they are a part (Wardyga, 2012).

## Accessing Cultural Content Using SNSs

Based on the interviewees' responses, the survey contained a question designed to determine what kind of topics participants often explored online (see Appendix B). Participants in the study reported that they used the internet to engage in exploration and commitment in a variety of ways, with most using the internet to access information about a variety of aspects of Korea, as reflected in Table 4.2 below. The vast majority of first-and-a-half generation participants and more than three quarters of second generation participants in the study consume not just a large amount of Korean entertainment media, but a large variety as well, including "Korean drama, variety/reality shows, movies, or clips" on the internet, which is consistent with the results of the PEIs. The first-and-a-half generation participants also reported exploring "news and current events in Korea" and "K-pop" as their second and third choice, while the second generation had a preference for "Korean celebrities" and "K-pop."

During the PEIs, as evidence of their connection with their ethnic identity, several interviewees reported that they are following Korean news stories as well as keeping up to date with K-pop, movies, and TV dramas using their digital media devices. Together, these activities seem to help these youths sustain their Korean language proficiency, but they simultaneously influence their ethnic identity in that these youths stay intimately connected to Korean culture while they are living in the U.S. Digital media thus allow for the various connections they have to their culture of origin, revealing how such technology plays a pivotal role in the interplay between the maintenance of a native language and the formation of an ethnic identity. For them, familiarity with Korean popular culture goes hand-in-hand with their ethnic identity formation since the former reflects an increased understanding of Korean culture and the Korean language, both of which they consider integral to their ethnic identity. What can be gleamed from the survey data and the PEI responses, then, is the implication that the specific sites that the children of Korean immigrants in the U.S. visit online in addition to the media that they consume on a daily basis may significantly influence the stability and fluidity of their ethnic identities (Mehra, Merkel, & Bishop, 2004).

It should be noted that while survey participants were given a set of choices for this survey question, those choices were developed based on the responses given by the 31 individuals who participated in the PEIs to the same question in an open-ended format; therefore, different data may have emerged if survey participants had been asked to respond spontaneously without being given a set of choices.

The survey also contained a question designed to determine how often participants watch Korean drama/movies (see Appendix B). Data from the survey indicated that about a third of participants watch Korean drama/movies at least

Table 4.2. Topics Explored on the Internet.

| | Generation Status | | |
|---|---|---|---|
| Topics explored on the internet | 1.5 (%) | 2nd (%) | Total (%) |
| Korean drama, variety/reality shows, movies, or clips | 27 (96.4) | 93 (78.8) | 120 (77.9) |
| K-pop | 21 (75) | 68 (54) | 89 (57.8) |
| Korean celebrities | 18 (64.3) | 51 (40.5) | 69 (44.8) |
| Korean clothing | 17 (60.7) | 30 (23.8) | 47 (30.5) |
| Korean food | 17 (60.7) | 50 (39.7) | 67 (43.5) |
| News and current events in Korea | 22 (78.6) | 48 (38.1) | 70 (45.45) |
| Information about Korean history | 5 (17.9) | 16 (12.7) | 21 (13.6) |
| Information about Korean religion | 3 (10.7) | 7 (5.6) | 10 (6.5) |
| Information about Korean holidays | 3 (10.7) | 13 (10.3) | 16 (10.4) |
| Information about Korean politics | 9 (32.1) | 20 (15.9) | 29 (18.8) |
| Information about Korean geography | 2 (7.1) | 7 (5.6) | 9 (5.8) |

occasionally or very frequently, not only demonstrating that more than one third of the participants in the study do consume Korean drama/movies, but also suggesting that such consumption reflects a certain degree of cultural interest that may influence how they negotiate their ethnic identities (see Table 4.3).

Throughout conversations during the PEIs, the interviewees used Korean drama/movies as proxies for describing their perceptions about their ethnic identities. Although the frequency of watching Korean drama/movies differs from one interviewee to another, most of them used their knowledge of drama/movies to support their claims of varying degrees of attachment to their ethnic identity. For some of the first-and-a-half generation interviewees, they feel that Korean drama/movies are a way for them to get back in touch with or remain connected to their homeland. For some of the second generation interviewees, since they are invested in exploring their ethnic identity, they are deeply and equally invested in learning about Korean drama/movies and in the meaning imbued in the time they spend with their family watching those dramas/movies. For them, Korean drama/movies are the one part of their ethnic identity that they eagerly explore. For several others, consumption of drama/movies and becoming knowledgeable about them are not only about a personal exploration, but are also based on what they believe their co-ethnic and non-Korean friends expect them to know about Korean popular culture.

For these Korean American children, Korean drama/movies appear to influence both how they see themselves in relation to their culture of origin and what they perceive their image to be to outsiders as well as to members of their ethnic communities. However, of 27 first-and-a-half generation survey participants, who claim to explore Korean drama, variety/reality shows, movies, or clips on the internet based on Table 4.3, three of them responded that they never watch Korean drama/movies on the Korean drama/movies frequency question. One explanation for this disparity might be related to the wording of the questions, specifically that "watching" Korean drama/movies could have been interpreted differently from "exploring" them on the internet.

Table 4.3. Frequency of Watching Korean Drama/Movies.

| | Generation Status | | |
|---|---|---|---|
| Frequency | 1.5 (%) | 2nd (%) | Total (%) |
| Never | 3 (10.7) | 31 (24.6) | 34 (22.1) |
| Very Rarely | 4 (14.3) | 17 (13.5) | 21 (13.6) |
| Rarely | 10 (35.7) | 36 (28.6) | 46 (29.9) |
| Occasionally | 6 (21.4) | 24 (19.1) | 30 (19.5) |
| Very Frequently | 5 (17.9) | 18 (14.3) | 23 (14.9) |
| Total | 28 (100) | 126 (100) | 154 (100) |

The survey further contained a question designed to determine how often participants watch Korean TV variety shows (see Appendix B). The results indicate that about half of the participants in this study watch Korean TV variety shows at least occasionally or very frequently, reflecting a cultural interest in such content that plays an influential role in their ethnic identity formation (see Table 4.4).

Throughout discussions during the PEIs, the most often mentioned element of Korean popular culture that pervaded most interviewees' descriptions of their media landscape was Korean TV variety shows. Interviewees routinely referenced their familiarity with Korean TV variety shows and displayed varying degrees of knowledge about them. When asked why they watch Korean TV variety shows, the overwhelming response from interviewees was that Korean TV variety shows are funnier than their American counterparts. Thus, not only do they connect on a deeper cultural level with Korean TV variety show content, but such content elicits more laughter than American variety shows. Furthermore, while some interviewees who distanced themselves from their ethnic identities often pointedly stated that they do not and never have watched Korean TV variety shows, the vast majority of those who did express a familiarity with them also claimed them as a marker of their ethnic identities.

However, of 27 first-and-a half generation participants who claimed to explore Korean drama, variety/reality shows, movies, or clips on the internet based on Table 3.1, one of them responded that he or she never watches Korean TV variety shows on the Korean TV variety show frequency question. One explanation for this again might be that the language of "watching" Korean TV variety shows was interpreted differently from "exploring" them on the internet.

Table 4.4. Frequency of Watching Korean TV Variety Shows.

| | Generation Status | | |
|---|---|---|---|
| Frequency | 1.5 (%) | 2nd (%) | Total (%) |
| Never | 2 (7.1) | 29 (23) | 31 (20.1) |
| Very Rarely | 4 (14.3) | 15 (11.1) | 19 (12.3) |
| Rarely | 6 (21.4) | 23 (18.3) | 29 (18.8) |
| Occasionally | 6 (21.4) | 30 (23.8) | 36 (23.4) |
| Very Frequently | 10 (35.7) | 29 (23) | 39 (25.3) |
| Total | 28 (100) | 126 (100) | 154 (100) |

As many interviewees would attest to during the PEIs, spending evenings glued to ethnic media content that provides the funniest entertainment, the hottest dramas, and the latest news as regular forms of cultural engagement is not simply a function of it being Korean, but is actually due to their own self-interests. As discussed in Chapter One, revolutions in digital media technologies shrink the constraints of time and space and enable these teens to consume their ethnic media in a shift away from traditional media to internet-based ones. As found in other studies showing the increasing trend of using smartphones instead of computers to go online (Yoon, 2016a, p. 7), the participants in this study are accessing the internet via their smartphones. For example, Yoon (2016b, p. 7) found that Korean immigrants in Canada generally used the internet, including hard-based downloading and streaming services, to view ethnic media. Park (2009, p. 137) and Son (2015, p. 388) also found that many Korean immigrant women were relying on the internet to watch Korean news, movies, and television. The same was true among our interviewees during the PEIs and survey participants, who are not only downloading K-pop and Korean movies but also watching Korean variety shows and dramas on the internet.

According to Yoon (2016b), some Korean immigrants in Canada had even committed daily and weekly television schedules to memory, suggesting that ethnic media content influenced their daily lives to a great extent. Considering their own media inclinations, this study's interviewees and survey participants have a choice between consuming host media or ethnic media. Among the various reasons for consuming their ethnic media, one key factor is that American media tends to misrepresent or underrepresent issues salient to their race or immigration status. Faced with such cultural marginalization, these children's consumption of ethnic media clearly helps them reinforce cultural connections and their ethnic identity. Indeed, ethnic media practices should be understood as coping mechanisms against racial and cultural exclusion in everyday life (Kim, 2011).

However, according to Metykova (2010), immigrants' daily activities with regard to digital media technologies are not revolutionary actions that emerged with immigration; many are instead carryovers from the home country. Those in the first-and-a half generation grew up with Korean media in Korea, indicating that digital media technologies brought continuity to their lives once they relocated to the host country. In their case, one of the important reasons for turning to ethnic media is to hold on to and continually revisit the memories of their childhood in their homeland. By further watching ethnic media's coverage of familiar places, faces, foods, and sounds, all of which are easily recognizable for them, they are able to reconnect with Korean culture and use it to alleviate feelings of homesickness.

In the case of second generation interviewees, one important function of ethnic media is the closing of any social gaps within their ethnic group. By watching Korean sitcoms, dramas, and movies and keeping abreast of popular Korean actors and news, they are not only able to build friendships and bond with co-ethnics, but that knowledge lessens the gap between the more ethnically oriented second generation individuals and the more assimilated Korean Americans (Oh, 2012, 2015). For example, while some are oriented towards Korea, others are oriented towards America. But no matter their orientation, by consuming ethnic media, they all demonstrate a social familiarity and bond with Korean culture. Therefore, by consuming the same ethnic media, even second generation children of Korean immigrants can adopt the latest sociocultural trends and shared tastes, not only helping them to possess a sense of belonging and commonality with the parents' home country (Park, 2004), but also serving as vehicles of cultural transmission to preserve their ethnic identity (Oh, 2012, 2015).

Nevertheless, the visibility with which these teens consume ethnic media using digital media technologies raises critical questions regarding the impact of that media on immigrants' adaptation to and integration with their places of settlement. On the one hand, ethnic media appeals to immigrants because they facilitate connections and keep them informed about current events in the home country (Elias, 2008). On the other hand, in their effort to stay relevant in the eyes of immigrants, ethnic media also engage in localization by providing valuable community information to support immigrant adaptation to the host country (Matsaganis, Ball-Rokeach, & Katz, 2011; Zhou & Cai, 2002). Ethnic media also help mitigate the isolation that immigrants face by ensuring a smooth transition into mainstream American society (Kim, 2011; Son, 2015; Zhou & Cai, 2002).

Among the criticisms of ethnic media consumption is the fear that immigrants, by staying connected to ethnic media content, are refusing assimilation and intentionally disengaging from the host country (Aksoy & Robins, 2000, p. 344). However, as Kim (2011) observes, while it does affect immigrants' attachment to and identification with the host country, consuming ethnic media is not synonymous with turning inward and rejecting the host culture. Despite public concerns that ethnic media may delay the assimilation of immigrants, particularly their learning English and establishing new relationships outside of their pre-established networks (Collins, 2009, p. 855), findings in this study from the PEIs and surveys frame the consumption of ethnic media via the latest digital technologies as a significant but neglected feature of these first-and-a half and second generation children of Korean immigrants. In fact, with growing ethnic media consumption via always-online smartphones, it may actually serve a dual function of assisting these teens' adaptation and integration while simultaneously giving them a means to stay connected to and to keep abreast of life in their home country.

In summary, the survey data show that these teens' pattern of media consumption differs considerably from that of the mainstream population, not unlike other immigrant families' different media consumption patterns as discussed in Lemish's (2007) research. Participants in this study regularly consume a wide variety of Korean media and expressed an affinity for programs ranging from Korean dramas to variety shows. This intense consumption ultimately indicates their intention to maintain and even strengthen ties with Korean popular culture, which in turn influences how they navigate their ethnic identity formation.

## SNSs as Ways of Maintaining Family Ties With Korea

In further discussions with several teenagers, other trends about their SNS use were also noteworthy. With the ubiquity of smartphones and internet access, new types of interpersonal relationships have emerged that allow these children of Korean immigrants to interact with others at any time. Similar to the popular adoption and usage of KakaoTalk discussed earlier in Chapter Two, smartphone-based communication helps to ease the separation between immigrant families and those family members still residing in the country of origin. Reflecting on her own personal involvement with SNSs, Jackie (15, F, City) said, "My family in the U.S. finds an easy and inexpensive way to take daily trips to Korea, to connect with family members far away and keep our relationship strong." When asked how they do it, she described how she and her family maintain contact with her cousin's family in Korea—through exchanging photographs and sending regular updates about family news and activities.

Here, Jackie aptly summarizes the far-reaching impact of SNSs on her life as well as on the lives of family members overseas. She pointed out that email had been her family's choice for keeping in touch with her relatives in Korea before SNSs. However, since the latter's arrival, it became her family's default communication platform, enabling them to talk to their relatives in Korea much more regularly than had been possible during the days of sending emails. The discussions she has with her relatives revolve mostly around everyday issues, although she did occasionally have serious discussions about her grandfather's death and cousin's wedding. Indeed, among the most important reasons for her family to increase communication with relatives in Korea through SNSs was, without a doubt, to maintain intimacy by sharing everyday life experiences from afar. As research shows, Skyping once a week with family members enables immigrants to establish a semblance of co-presence among them despite a physical separation (Nedelcu, 2012).

As one example of this family sharing and exchange, she showed a picture of herself with her family that she posted on her Facebook page to allow her cousin's family to experience her life and interact with her by leaving comments. (see Figure 4.7)

She continued,

> This is a picture of my family at a ceremony where I received an award. It's one of many that I posted on Facebook for my cousin's family to see. I post lots of pictures of

> regular events such as what we're eating or reading and special events attended by our family, like concerts and parties. They were very proud to see me holding my award at the ceremony, and they wrote, "Wow! Congratulations on your award! What an accomplishment! No one deserves this award more than you. We're so proud!" I also chat with my favorite cousin to say "Hello," check out some of his photos on Facebook, and comment on new pictures by saying that he looks good or funny. I have several cousins, but he's like a brother to me. Looking at his pictures reminds me of the time we spent together when I visited Korea a few years ago.

Jackie's engagement with SNSs seems to allow her and her family to invite their extended family members overseas to continue being an essential part of their daily lives and to prevent family fragmentation despite the great geographical distance.

Jackie was not alone, however, in using SNSs as a tool to strengthen relationships with extended family members overseas. According to Mijung (16, F, Metro), she set up a Facebook account for her mother so that she could stay connected with her family by posting photos. She said, "I opened a Facebook account for my mom because she wants to post our family pictures for many extended family members to see, like her parents and my dad's parents." It seems that even physical, geographical distance does not remove the firmly held family obligation to stay in regular touch, because family links are stronger among Koreans than any other links (Fortunati, Pertierra, & Vincent, 2012).

Because our interview sample included a number of first-and-a half generation youths, who had spent their formative years in Korea and second generation youths, who are interested in their parents' culture due to being born in the U.S., several actually mentioned travelling to Korea from time to time as part of their family activities. Those who have managed to visit Korea did so for different reasons, including attending summer culture/language camp or for a family member's wedding or death. In terms of the frequency of their visits, owing to the distance between their current location and Korea, many expressed difficulty in finding both the time and the money to make repeated trips to Korea. Yet, access to SNSs and apps such as KakaoTalk in turn granted more regular contact with family and friends in Korea without having to wait for the once-a-year or once-every-few-years visit. In fact, Mijung's most recent "trip" to Korea was on the morning before the interview day, when she and her mother used Facebook to connect with their family abroad.

Jackie's and Mijung's cases speak to the views of other interviewees who also explained how their engagement with SNSs counteracts geographical distance as it both foregrounds and strengthens bonds with family members or friends who are scattered across the globe. They corroborated how SNSs allow families and friends separated by distance to be emotionally involved in each other's lives and subsequently feel strong connections across borders. While the need to keep intimacy with family members is a major driver of SNS usage among these interviewees, other factors such as entertainment and news (information), familiarity, and continuity, among others, are also behind the adoption and use of digital media technologies and their apps. One such example comes from Emily (14, F, Rural). "Every day when I get home from school, one of the first things I do is turn on my computer, log in to Facebook, and talk with my friend Alex in Korea using Facebook's webcam," she said. (see Figure 4.8)

She continued,

> After a few minutes, Alex connects and appears on the screen from Korea. Then, we start to chat in English because Alex was also born in the United States just like me and moved to Korea with his family. He was a good friend of mine when he was here, but I feel we are still good friends because we talk every day.

After Alex returned to Korea, it was initially difficult for her to see him face-to-face or even call him. Without the digital media technology that she uses so much today, she and Alex would have to rely on sending the occasional letter or making sporadic phone calls, which could result in their friendship eroding over time. Social networking, and all of the communicative possibilities therein, has therefore become central to how Emily and Alex maintain their friendship even as they grow up in different countries.

When describing their online conversations, Emily said that the content includes not only discussions of news and current events in America, but also the various happenings in Korea, as well as discussions of their now different school lives. She also reported that what motivated her to consume more Korean media was Alex himself, who acted as her window to life in Korea, a country she has never visited. This cultural exchange is actually bi-directional, for just as Alex is her gateway to Korean popular culture, including K-pop, sports, entertainment, and even celebrity gossip, she is his gateway to the same kind of content from America. Through regular online conversations, which has become part of their daily activities, the circulation of cultural and social norms and values is visible in their interactions as Alex in Korea shares Korean culture and language with Emily, while Emily in the U.S. in turn shares up-to-date information on American schools, social life, and sports with Alex, illustrating mutually rewarding online communication and interaction (Nedelcu, 2012, p. 14).

Although Wilding (2006, p.132) argues that the exchange, not the content, is central to online conversations because it helps sustain intimacy among immigrants, Emily's case highlights the content of online exchanges as playing a key role in fulfilling both individuals' cultural interests as well as strengthening their personal, emotional ties. By using their familiarity with either Korean or American popular culture as a form of cultural capital, sharing it with one another then validates their relationship as one of mutual cultural interest that influences their ethnic identities. For them, web links, K-pop, news stories, and photos shared with each other through Facebook chats help to develop what is known in research as "the mundane," resulting in ongoing communication despite the physical distance (Metykova, 2010).

Although the degree of SNS engagement differs from one user to another, social networking in general has become integral to keeping intact and even expanding diverse social and cultural links to Korea, and vice versa, among the interviewees. Jackie's, Mijung's, and Emily's cases, most specifically, suggest strong evidence for the revolutionary potential of SNSs to mimic the kind of face-to-face socialization that occurs in the average Korean American teen's real world, especially when that kind of socialization is physically impossible due to geographical distance. Therefore, although these teens live life in their local communities, they flexibly navigate two different cultural spaces using SNSs. Such flexible navigation via SNSs, especially their inseparable connection with Korea through frequent and intimate communicative exchanges with friends and family, may alter their perception of their everyday local life as it allows them to incorporate Korean cultural elements into and even extend their ethnic identities in increasingly unique and significant ways.

As listed in Table 4.5 below, survey participants in the study use a variety of social media sites. It should be noted that the participants had the option of responding to all that applies among multiple categories. On one hand, the vast majority of first-and-a-half generation participants reported that they use Facebook first and YouTube second as their social media sites. Facebook thus emerged as the most frequently used social media site for this group (see Table 4.5). On the other hand, the order flipped for second generation participants, with the vast majority reporting that they use YouTube the most, followed by Facebook. YouTube thus emerged as this group's most frequently used social media site.

However, when looking at the participants in total without considering their generation status, the vast majority use YouTube as their most common social media site for their social media practices; among all 154 participants,

140 (90.9%) reported that they use YouTube as their social media site. YouTube is a video-sharing website on which anyone can upload content that everyone else can then view, and as one of the most visited and widely used streaming video sites on the internet, YouTube lies at the intersection of media creation and social networking, providing young people with a participatory culture in which to create and share original content while making new social connections (Chau, 2010).

During the PEIs, many interviewees found YouTube to be a better source of video entertainment than other sites. One characteristic of the website that they singled out was its relatively limited barriers, which both simplify everything from account creation to uploading and viewing content and facilitate community engagement even at the periphery. According to the interviewees, most of them are unregistered YouTube users who simply enjoy viewing videos. Their specific reasons for visiting YouTube range from wanting to be entertained, to pass time, to watch videos, to keep up with what their friends are watching and talking about, and to follow up on videos recommended by their friends. When they were asked to describe the most frequent types of videos they watch on YouTube, Korean media entertainment videos—including Korean drama/movies, variety/reality shows, K-pop videos, and news about Korean celebrities—received the most emphatic responses. For instance, Ye Seul provided a good example of this practice in describing how she watches Korean dramas on YouTube before then sharing her favorite Korean dramas with her other co-ethnic friends afterward.

In discussions of their primary uses of YouTube, many of the interviewees are relying on YouTube via their smartphones to consume K-pop. While Facebook is generally reserved for Korean immigrants to search for or participate in social events in the host society (Yoon, 2016b, p. 9), YouTube seems to be the most popular site for these children of Korean immigrants to follow K-pop. The responses from the interviewees suggest that many of them have made following K-pop a highly routinized daily ritual. Given the undeniable influence that K-pop has had in putting Korea and Korean culture on the global stage, as was described in Chapter Two, the impact of the Korean Wave on both the first-and-a-half and second generations is even more striking. With the unbelievable success of Psy's popular music video, *Gangnam Style* on YouTube (1.5 billion views) and in the U.S. music scene, K-pop is clearly captivating these groups.

Contrary to our expectation that the impact of K-pop on the second generation would be minimal when compared to that on the first-and-a-half generation, even the former reported strong feelings of pride as Korean

Americans due to the increased name recognition of well-known K-pop stars. With Korea's newfound prominence in global culture and world affairs, they no longer have to point out to their friends where exactly Korea is located on a world map during conversations. In fact, several of the second generation interviewees acknowledged that Korea's improved image—thanks to the rising popularity of K-pop—has positively affected their ethnic identity development. This phenomenon, manifest in a deep interest in K-pop, especially among the second generation, underscores the role of YouTube, made only more accessible with the widespread adoption of smartphones.

Consistent with discussions during the PEIs, Table 4.1, previously discussed above, shows the variety of Korean media entertainment programs that survey participants most often explore online. As YouTube was found to be participants' most frequented social media site, the result suggests that YouTube may also be the most frequented platform that they use for exploring or consuming their Korean media entertainment. Therefore, as is evident from the PEIs and survey responses, YouTube has become an integral site for these teens in that it fosters feelings of belonging and encourages ethnic identity exploration precisely because it allows them to create personal spaces filled with meaningful texts and makes it simple to then share all that they create (Chau, 2010).

The next most frequented social media site was Facebook, with a vast majority of the youth reporting that they use it as their social media site. These results indicate that the participants in the study not only rely on YouTube for their social media needs, but that they simultaneously access Facebook. After all, Facebook's 89.0% access rate was almost equivalent to YouTube's 90.9%. A strong preference for Facebook and its robust social networking features also emerged among a majority of the interviewees during the PEIs. Some explained that they felt Facebook was preferable because of its more thorough privacy settings. For example, Jieun (17, F, City) described Facebook as "more sophisticated" than MySpace because on Facebook, she is aware of exactly who is sending her friend requests. In contrast, MySpace makes her profile public to the point that random strangers tend to send her friend requests. Some interviewees voluntarily joined Facebook because their friends had, while others reported that they did so as a result of peer pressure. Yet, regardless of their reasons for joining, because of its reputation as a more private networking space, Facebook enjoys greater popularity among young Korean Americans compared to other SNSs.

As discussed previously regarding Table 4.4, most of the participants, regardless of generation status, use Facebook as their most frequent text messaging application in their daily social interactions. During the PEIs, one interesting trend that was revealed about interviewees' smartphone practices is how their social interactions involve not only text messaging, but also the exchange of various media, such as photos, videos, and other content. By uploading that content to Facebook in the context of that site's virtual socialization, interviewees learn creative new ways to explore and take ownership of their ethnic backgrounds as they negotiate their ethnic identities by browsing the vast amount of media shared by others. Moreover, this virtual socialization also grants them numerous opportunities to show interest in the media they consume as expressions of their ethnic identity (Liu, 2007).

Another interesting trend that was noticed across several interviewees is their way of communicating and maintaining family ties and social relationships across borders by taking advantage of virtual socialization through SNSs. Based on their responses, their SNSs, particularly Facebook, allow them to keep their family or friends overseas as an essential part of their daily lives and prevent family fragmentation among them despite the obvious geographical distance. Staying up to date with Korean popular culture materials, such as K-pop, sports, entertainment, and even celebrity gossip, is the interviewees' way of sustaining emotional ties and cultural expectations with co-ethnic friends with whom they are in regular contact through SNSs or even with other family members and friends in Korea.

While, according to the survey results, the second most frequented social media site is Facebook, the results do not indicate for what purposes participants use Facebook. However, with the benefits of having conducted PEIs and having uncovered rich stories and examples of how participants derive meaning from their social media interactions, it is suggested that Facebook gives the children of Korean immigrants in this study a powerful means to maintain an inseparable connection with Korea through frequent and intimate communicative exchanges with friends and family. As a result of this "keeping feet in both worlds" (Levitt, 2003, p. 177) through Facebook, they have the power to incorporate Korean cultural elements into and even extend their ethnic identities in increasingly unique and significant ways.

Due to constant innovations in digital media technologies and the ease of access to ethnic media content, both of which enable increased social and cultural engagement with the homeland, these children of Korean immigrants do not rely exclusively on a single digital media device. Rather, they integrate various digital media devices into their lives to stay connected with the homeland on two fronts: through media consumption and intense engagement with SNSs and personal communication applications (Madianou & Miller, 2012,

Table 4.5. Types of Social Media.

| | Generation Status | | |
|---|---|---|---|
| Social Media | 1.5 (%)<br>n = 28 | 2nd (%)<br>n = 126 | Total (%)<br>N = 154 |
| YouTube | 24 (85.7) | 116 (92.1) | 140 (90.9) |
| Facebook | 27 (96.4) | 110 (87.3) | 137 (89) |
| Instagram | 8 (28.6) | 64 (50.8) | 72 (46.7) |
| Twitter | 5 (17.8) | 19 (15.1) | 24 (15.6) |
| Tumblr | 0 | 23 (18.2) | 23 (14.3) |
| Pinterest | 3 (10.7) | 9 (7.1) | 12 (7.8) |
| Reddit | 1 (3.6) | 6 (4.8) | 5 (4.5) |
| MySpace | 0 | 2 (1.6) | 2 (1.3) |
| Others | 2 (7.1) | 5 (4) | 7 (4.5) |

*Others (specify): LOL, KakaoTalk, Snapchat, KakaoStory, agag, Viber, Yelp, and Vine.

p. 3). This means that the culture gap is likely to decrease to where there are no discernible differences in how quickly and extensively K-pop culture gets consumed by the first-and-a-half and second generations. Given the responses from the interviewees and survey outcomes, it is safe to say that this group is likely to stay oriented towards their culture of origin, deepening their cultural engagement with the home country for the foreseeable future. It can therefore be argued that the increasing adoption of smartphones, with their computing power, network connectivity, and portability, undeniably brought into their lives a tendency towards bicultural orientation.

## References

Aksoy, A., & Robins, K. (2000). Thinking across spaces: Transnational television from Turkey. *European Journal of Cultural Studies*, 3(3), 343–365.

Bae, M. S. (2010). Go Cyworld! Korean diasporic girls producing new Korean femininity. In S. R. Mazzarella (Ed.), *Girl Wide Web 2.0: Revisiting girls, the Internet, and the negotiation of identity* (pp. 91–116). New York, NY: Peter Lang.

Bandon, A. (1994). *Korean Americans*. New York, NY: New Discovery.

boyd, d. m. (2007). Why youth (heart) social network sites: The role of networked publics in teenage social life. In D. Buckingham (Ed.), *Youth, identity, and digital media* (pp. 119–142). Cambridge, MA: MIT Press.

Chau, C. (2010). YouTube as a participatory culture. *New Directions for Youth Development, 2010*(128), 65–74. doi: 10.1002/yd.376

Chen, W. (2009). *Internet use and intercultural adaptation: A case study on Chinese immigrants in Singapore*. Paper presented at the annual meeting of the International Communication Association, New York City, NY.

Collins, F. (2009). Connecting home with here: Personal homepages in everyday transnational lives. *Journal of Ethnic and Migration Studies*, *35*(6), 839–859.

Elias, N. (2008). *Coming home: Media and returning diaspora in Israel and Germany*. Albany, NY: State University of New York Press.

Fortunati, D., Pertierra, R., & Vincent, J. (2012). *Migration, diaspora, and information technology in global societies*. New York, NY: Routledge.

Gans, H. J. (2004). The American kaleidoscope, then and now. In T. Jacoby (Ed.), *Reinventing the melting pot: The new immigrants and what it means to be American* (pp. 33–45). New York, NY: Basic Books.

Illouz, E. (2007). *Cold intimacies: The making of emotional capitalism*. Cambridge, UK: Polity Press.

Kim, Y. (2011). *Transnational migration, media and identity of Asian women: Diasporic daughters*. London: Routledge.

Lee, R. M. (2003). Do ethnic identity and other-group orientation protect against discrimination for Asian Americans? *Journal of Counseling Psychology*, *50*(2), 133–141.

Lee, S. K., & Katz, J. E. (2015). Bounded solidarity confirmed? How Korean immigrants' mobile communication configures their social networks. *Journal of Computer-Mediated Communication*, *20*(6), 615–631.

Lemish, D. (2007). *Children and television: A global perspective*. Malden, MA: Blackwell Publishing.

Lehrer, B. (1996). *The Korean Americans*. New York, NY: Chelsea House.

Levitt, P. (2003). Keeping feet in both worlds: Transnational practices and immigration incorporation in the United States. In C. Joppke & E. Morawska (Eds.), *Toward assimilation and citizenship: Immigrants in liberal nation-states* (pp. 177–194). New York, NY: Palgrave MacMillan.

Liu, H. (2007). Social network profiles as taste performances. *Journal of Computer-Mediated Communication*, *13*(1), 252–275.

Madianou, M., & Miller, D. (Eds.). (2012). *Migration and new media: Transnational families and polymedia*. London: Routledge.

Mansumitrchai, S., Park, C.-H., & Chiu, C. L. (2012). Factors underlying the adoption of social network: A study of Facebook users in South Korea. *International Journal of Business and Management*, *7*(24), 138–153.

Marcia, J. (1980). Identity in adolescence. In J. Adelson (Ed.), *Handbook of adolescent psychology* (pp. 159–187). New York, NY: Wiley.

Matsaganis, M. D., Ball-Rokeach, S. J., & Katz, V. S. (2011). *Understanding ethnic media: Producers, consumers, and societies*. Thousand Oaks, CA: Sage.

Mehra, B., Merkel, C., & Bishop, A. P. (2004). The Internet for empowerment of minority and marginalized users. *New Media & Society*, *6*(6), 781–802.

Metykova, M. (2010). Only a mouse click away from home: Transnational practices of Eastern European migrants in the United Kingdom. *Social Identities*, *16*(3), 325–338.

Min, P. G. (2002). Introduction. In P. G. Min (Ed.), *The second generation: Ethnic identity among Asian Americans* (pp. 1–14). Walnut Creek, CA: AltaMira Press.

Min, P. G., & Kim, R. (2000). Formation of ethnic and racial identities: Narratives by young Asian-American professionals. *Ethnic and Racial Studies*, *23*(4), 735–760.

Nedelcu, M. (2012). Migrants' new transnational habitus: Rethinking, migration through a cosmopolitan lens in the digital age. *Journal of Ethnic and Migration Studies*, *38*(9), 1339–1356.

Oh, D. (2012). Mediating the boundaries: Second-generation Korean American adolescents' use of transnational Korean media as markers of social boundaries. *International Communication Gazette*, *74*(3), 258–276.

Oh, D. (2015). *Second-generation Korean Americans and transnational media: Diasporic identifications*. Lanham, MD: Lexington Books.

Oh, J.-H. (2016a). Immigration and social capital in a Korean-American women's online community: Supporting acculturation, cultural pluralism, and transnationalism. *New Media & Society*, *18*(10), 2224–2241.

Oh, J.-H. (2016b). *Immigration and social capital in the age of social media*. Lanham, MD: Lexington.

Panagakos, A. (2003). Downloading new identities: Ethnicity, technology, and media in the global Greek village. *Identities: Global Studies in Culture and Power*, *10*, 201–219.

Park, J.-S. (2004). Korean American youth and transnational flows of popular culture across the Pacific. *Amerasia Journal*, *30*, 147–169.

Park, S. (2009). Negotiating identities and re-acculturation of second-generation Korean Americans: The role of ethnic media and peer group dynamics. *Korea Journal*, *49*(1), 61–97.

Phinney, J., & Ong, A. (2007). Conceptualization and measurement of ethnic identity: Current status and future directions. *Journal of Counseling Psychology*, *54*(3), 271–281.

Portes, A., & Zhou, M. (1993). The new second generation: Segmented assimilation and its variants. *Annals of the American Academy of Political and Social Science*, *530*, 74–96.

Rosen, L. D. (2010). *Rewired: Understanding the igeneration and the way they learn*. New York, NY: Palgrave Macmillan.

Son, J. (2015). Immigrant incorporation, technology, and transnationalism among Korean American women. *Journal of International Migration and Integration*, *16*, 377–395.

Song, A. M. (2003). *Choosing ethnic identity*. Cambridge, UK: Polity Press.

Tajfel, H., & Turner, J. (1986). The social identity theory of intergroup behavior. In S. Worchel & W. Austin (Eds.), *Psychology of intergroup relations* (pp. 7–24). Chicago, IL: Nelson-Hall.

Thai, H. C. (2002). Formation of ethnic identity among second-generation Vietnamese Americans. In P. G. Min (Ed.), *The second generation: Ethnic identity among Asian Americans* (pp. 53–83). Walnut Creek, CA: AltaMira Press.

Wardyga, B. J. (2012). *The relationship between text message volume and formal writing performance among upper level high school students and college freshmen*. (Doctoral dissertation). Retrieved from http://digitalcommons.liberty.edu/cgi/viewcontent.cgi?article=1577&context=doctoral

Wilding R. (2006). Virtual intimacies? Families communicating across transnational contexts. *Global Networks*, *6*(2), 125–142.

Yoon, K. (2016a). The cultural appropriation of smartphones in Korean transnational families. In S. S. Lim (Ed.), *Mobile communication and the family: Asian experiences in technology domestication* (pp. 93–108). New York, NY: Springer.

Yoon, K. (2016b). Korean migrants' use of the Internet in Canada. *Journal of International Migration and Integration*, *18*(2), 547–562.

Zhou, M., & Cai, G. (2002). Chinese language media in the United States: Immigration and assimilation in American life. *Qualitative Sociology*, *25*(3), 419–441.

Figure 4.1. Having SNSs Available on My Smartphone.
Source: Photo by Hye Jin.

Figure 4.2. White Christmas Day.
Source: Photo by Hye Jin.

Figure 4.3. My Cash Gift *Suhl-Nahl.*
Source: Photo by Hye Jin.

Figure 4.4. My Bi-cultural Social Circle.
Source: Photo by Jackie.

Figure 4.5. My First Local Co-ethnic Friend.
Source: Photo by Annie.

Figure 4.6. Korean Candies.
Source: Photo by Jimmy.

Figure 4.7. My Family at the Award Ceremony.
Source: Photo by Jackie.

Figure 4.8. Chatting Through Facebook's Webcam.
Source: Photo by Emily.

· 5 ·

# NAVIGATING KOREAN AND AMERICAN IDENTITIES

We turn now to the discussion of the third research question of this study: how does digital media consumption affect this young population's assimilation into mainstream American society? The use of digital media to negotiate between two cultures and two sets of identities, what previous researchers defined as an "inward-outward" relationship, is at the core of the discussion in this chapter. Issues related to maintaining proficiency in both Korean and English languages is at the heart of this challenge, both very much in line with previous immigration studies yet shaped differently due to the availability of digital media. Consuming and enjoying K-pop (i.e., Korean pop culture) in addition to mainstream western pop is another manifestation of this ability to reside within two locales at the same time.

The children interviewed in this study occupy two different places along the spectrum of personal immigration status as previously defined in the literature section: first-and-a-half generation and second generation Korean American children. On one hand, first-and-a-half generation Korean American children are of particular interest in this study because they have spent at least some of their formative years in both Korea and the U.S., long enough to know both cultures. Although they share similar characteristics with their second generation counterparts, who were born to immigrant parents in the U.S., they brought with them a diverse blend of linguistic, cultural, and social beliefs and practices when they came to the U.S. On the other hand, second generation interviewees are equally important in this study in that their exposure to American culture from birth is what initially informs their identity construction. All interviewees in this study, whether first-and-a-half or second generation, shared everything from short anecdotes to more in-depth explanations in explaining how their self-descriptions vary.

Descendants of immigrants face distinctive challenges owing to the experience of acculturation and tensions that arise from the dynamics of choosing between a freely chosen identity and social acceptance. As expected, identity conflict or struggle was a common experience for nearly all interviewees at least "at some point" in their lives. For instance, using a red fish in his image as a compelling metaphor, Eddie (16, M, Metro) described his contradictory cultural worlds and the struggle he faces to capture meaning in his experiences of inhabiting both. (see Figure 5.1)

> This is … I couldn't really take a picture … This image is more like my feelings now. This [red fish] would be me, and the other fish are just everybody else. I am trying to fit in with everyone else and be included with everyone, but it is kind of challenging. Sometimes, I feel different [in the picture, only the red fish moves from right to left, the opposite of every other fish]. Because I'm between these two different cultures, I feel like I have both an American side and a Korean side. Sometimes, when I mix them, I feel perfectly normal. But, at other times, I feel different because I feel like I don't belong to either.

Eddie's quote adequately summarizes many interviewees' past or ongoing identity struggles that they have faced at some point in their lives. Of course, these interviewees vary across several dimensions regarding their background, such as birth place, length of residence in America, family dynamic, community dynamic, and their degree of contact with co-ethnic friends or individuals in their homeland. Some interviewees come from a privileged background, which includes highly educated parents, while others, whose parents are less educated and thus struggling with lower incomes, face challenges associated with poverty. However, in the event that cultural or social contradictions arise in interviewees' lives, they often grow concerned about their ethnic identities since identity stands out in the face of such strong contradictions.

## Ethnic Identity Development Among First-and-a-Half Generation Interviewees

Ha Sun (17, F, Metro) describes identity struggles similar to Eddie's. She is one of the first-and-a-half generation interviewees in this study, and she claims to stay in constant touch with her homeland. In her interview, she recalled her feelings of the first few weeks at school after arriving to the U.S. from Korea at the age of 11.

> No matter how you look at it, leaving Korea for the U.S. in order to begin a new life was the most stressful and life-changing event I have ever had to go through. I had to learn an unfamiliar school system, a new culture, a new language, and make new friends. At the same time, I was losing many of my closest relationships, including with my relatives and friends, back in Korea. I felt like I didn't belong, like I was suffering a real sense of loss.

Ha Sun's statement reveals a unique aspect of many first-and-a-half generation interviewees' immigrant experiences in that they must adjust to American culture during childhood, while second generation interviewees reported little difficulty adopting American cultures, values, norms, and beliefs. The side effect that Ha Sun describes of losing the close, personal communication she had with family and friends back in her home country also contrasts with American-born interviewees in this study, who did not spend their formative years in Korea and therefore have not experienced such significant separations during childhood from those closest to them. Ha Sun's initial period of immigration was thus characterized by an identity struggle compounded by a feeling of not belonging.

However, despite Ha Sun's difficulties, at the time of the interview, she displayed a resilient attitude. When asked whether she still faced the same difficulties now, she described how she dealt with her stress by actively engaging with her home country using SNSs via her smartphone and how this engagement counteracted the distance and lessened her feeling of homesickness. As she said, "Not really … School was the place where I learned about American culture and American life, but Facebook is how I stay in touch with relatives and friends back home and feel closer, more connected to them." Despite few close relationships with local peers, her daily connections with family and friends in Korea via SNSs, fueled by feelings of nostalgia for her homeland, act as a kind of antidote to the tensions caused by the struggle to adapt to a new environment. Indeed, research literature highlights this very kind of emotional support, in which an immigrant child's ties with family and friends in the homeland are rebuilt in a digital space, leading to a more stable adjustment in their new country of residence (Fogt & Sandvik, 2008).

In terms of her ethnic identity, Ha Sun used to feel culturally torn during her initial period of adaptation, but she now feels more Korean than American and enthusiastically claims her Koreanness by showing one of her Facebook photos. She said, "This is a Korean map. The reason I took a picture of a Korean map is because it is my original birthplace. I still miss familiar Korean culture and places and my previous social circles …" Her current home may be America, but Ha Sun's picture of a Korean map indicates that she does not orient herself toward America. Rather, Korea is the foundation of her identity. (see Figure 5.2)

When asked further about the meaning of this photo, she replied,

> While travelling, if someone asks me "What country are you from," I naturally answer, "I am originally from Korea." I guess that my gut feeling tells me that I am a Korean … This map reminds me of my roots, where I came from … Korea is without a doubt my home country.

During her interview, she frequently referenced Korea in very personal terms, using descriptions such as "my home country." This kind of language suggests that Ha Sun's connection to Korea as her home country is more than just a strong attachment; it is a kind of ownership. She identifies as Korean and claims Korea, instead of her current country of residence, as her home. In this context, the photo serves as the focal point of her ethnic identity. Furthermore, in stating Korea as her birthplace to diverse individuals when travelling, she travels as a Korean and a representative of its culture.

Not only was Ha Sun the only interviewee in this study who claimed a Korean ethnic identity, but her professed Koreanness remained firm regardless of whether she resided in Korea or America. When asked about the role of digital media in preserving her Korean ethnic identity, she said,

> I guess it did play an important role … My SNSs are like a fast-moving jet that can take me back to Korea anytime I want to go. They help me stay connected to my birthplace, where my Korean identity was born.

Ethnic identity may have been location-specific in the past for many people, but Ha Sun's quote demonstrates that in this era of digital media technology, distance does not necessarily diminish one's cultural connection to their birthplace. Her Koreanness is not simply alive after her immigration to America, it has solidified. Ha Sun's case shows not only the way SNSs play a major role in reconnecting her with her homeland, but also in giving her an outlet to express what she values in terms of her ethnic identity, such as a photo of her Korean map. This virtual network of constant interaction with her homeland appears to form the fundamental foundation of her unshaken Korean identity, an identity similar to those of her compatriots who still reside in Korea.

Unlike Ha Sun, who favors a Korean identity over an American one, another first-and-a-half generation interviewee, Suji (15, F, Metro), interestingly discussed how two different pictures that she had posted on her Facebook page represent her sophisticated cultural and social worlds. She said, "This is a picture of my favorite drink. It's a white chocolate mocha from Starbucks. When I hang out with my American school friends, I prefer to stop by Starbucks with them and drink a white chocolate mocha."

She then showed the other picture, which represented a different cultural and social context. "When I hang out with my Korean church friends, I sometimes choose instead to drop by a Korean dessert shop with them and have *potbingsoo*, a Korean popular dessert." According to her, she grew up eating *potbingsoo* with her childhood friends while residing in Korea. For her, it seems that eating *potbingsoo* with her co-ethnic friends at the local Korean dessert shop in the U.S. reminds her of her home, Korea. (see Figure 5.3)

The pictures themselves are meaningful, but so were the comments she received from her friends.

> When I uploaded the picture of *potbingsoo*, my Korean church friends wrote comments like, "Yeah, we enjoyed doing this together," "I miss the taste of *potbingsoo* from when I was in Korea," and "Oh … I miss Korea." But, my American friends' comments were quite different. Their comments were, "I've never tried it before. What is it," "Hum … it looks weird," and "Let me try one." I like reading all my friends' comments, and I'm sure you can see how they respond differently to the same picture.

According to her, the photo of *potbingsoo* was greeted with positive, empathetic comments from her co-ethnic friends since they, too, were familiar with its taste and cultural connotation. For Suji, then, eating *potbingsoo* is a nostalgic act, and sharing the photo online creates an opportunity to connect with her co-ethnic friends who also associate *potbingsoo* with their childhoods.

When examined in the context of Livingstone (2008), SNSs become outlets of expression in which Suji is visible to her friends and where she can experiment with projections of herself based on her peers' reactions. Suji's use of the word "different" to describe her American friends' reactions to the photo of *potbingsoo* compared with those of her co-ethnic friends seems to imply that the former group lacks the cultural context necessary to truly understand Koreans' nostalgic connection to such cultural elements as *potbingsoo*. It is noteworthy, however, that her SNSs contain photos of both American and Korean cultural elements, thus playing a vital role in helping her build "a newly emerging hybrid cultural realm" (Elias & Lemish, 2008,

p. 173), one that blends aspects of both cultures into a personalized mixture of American and Korean influences.

When Suji was asked to explain further what these two different photos represented to her, she said,

> Although my Korean church friends and I are white-washed, we are still influenced by our parents and our childhoods. I really like American food, but I just can't live without Korean food. For example, I can't eat burgers for three straight days. I need to eat Korean food regularly as well. So, my mom cooks Korean food at least one time a day. For example, breakfast usually includes things like cereal, tomato soup, bread, or omelets. Then, school lunch is usually something like a sandwich. When I come back from school, then we eat Korean food for dinner. With my Korean church friends, it's the same kind of routine. We do eat American food most of the time, but sometimes we just need to avoid it. So, we occasionally go to a Korean restaurant or Korean dessert shop.

According to Lee (2003), consuming ethnic food can be viewed as an expression of one's ethnic identity. Suji is therefore expressing her Koreanness in her emotional discussion of needing to eat Korean food as a nostalgic bridge to her homeland.

In her comparisons, Suji used two different pictures to explain the two different cultural and social worlds that she values. On one hand, the picture of a white chocolate mocha from Starbucks allows her to express what she values in terms of her American cultural and social world. On the other hand, the picture of *potbingsoo* allows for the same with regards to her Korean cultural and social world. Both photos thus appear to serve as reference points for different facets of her ethnic identity. Indeed, most evident from her interview is how she uses SNSs to reconcile the two different cultures of which she is a part, projecting certain elements of her identity in the form of text or photos in order to showcase what matters to her or to present herself in a way that she finds most desirable.

According to Suji, her daily activities and social interactions take place primarily with her American friends. She enjoys hanging out with them at school and in daily life, meaning that she does not restrict herself to activities and social interactions within the Korean community. Instead, she seems to feel very comfortable with both cultures and even continues to maintain a sense of continuity with familiar cultural practices that she used to enjoy in Korea before her immigration, such as having *potbingsoo* at a local Korean dessert shop while living in the U.S. As she said during her interview, "Although I have been living in the U.S. for three years, I have tried to live a Korean lifestyle even though I'm surrounded by American culture." She may live like a Korean with respect to regular food consumption and certain aspects of her lifestyle, but her cultural orientation is bi-directional and depends on the particular cultural and social circumstances in which she finds herself. In other words, she may identify more with one culture at any given moment, but the overall picture that she paints is one of flexible bi-cultural orientation, which allows her to synthesize her two different cultural frameworks within her overall ethnic identity (Akhtar, 2011).

Mari (15, F, City) described her own bi-cultural orientation that is quite similar to Suji's.

> This picture shows my friends and me studying. Although we study and talk in English, you can see some Korean culture when you look at our pencil cases. We like Korean stuff very much, especially fashion and accessories. When I come back to the U.S. from Korea with my family, I often buy Korean products at the airport and upload pictures of them on my Facebook page … For example, all my friends loved these pencil cases because they show off a traditional Korean style with a trendy look. We also regularly go shopping at local Korean stores and post pictures on Facebook of things that we buy. We then use the pictures to exchange things. If one of us is interested in something that we post a picture of, we loan it out so others can use it for a while and return it later. (see Figure 5.4)

As illustrated above in the photo, even though Mari overcame several challenges of adjusting to life in the U.S., such as culture shock and language barriers, and became well-integrated into the American school system, she still demonstrates a strong preference for Korean cultural commodities when shopping because of her familiarity with them as a child in Korea. According to her, she also browses commercial websites that sell modern Korean-style clothes to update herself on the latest fashion trends. Such online activities help build the foundation of her bonds with her co-ethnic friends who likewise cherish and consume the same products.

Mari's SNS use is of course influenced by American culture, but there is also a noticeable Korean influence in her interactions. Besides consuming Korean cultural commodities, Mari reported that she routinely watches Korean dramas on YouTube using her tablet because watching Korean dramas with her family was a cherished family activity in Korea. She said,

> Watching Korean dramas on YouTube is my way to get back in touch with my homeland. If I like a particular drama that I watch, I copy the link and post it on my Facebook page … I love to see all the likes and to see the counter increase as more people click the link.

By consuming dramas, she maintains a sense of continuity—even while living in the U.S.—with familiar cultural practices that she enjoyed with her family back in Korea. Then, by extending her viewing habits and preferences to Facebook, she creates her own interactive space of socialization where she can allow her peers to witness, understand, and even participate in the Korean aspects of her ethnic identity.

During the interview, she said that because she faces the challenge of being "American" in front of her American friends at school and "Korean" in front of her co-ethnic peers in her ethnic community, she identifies herself as a Korean American. She also described how she and her co-ethnic friends use Korean cultural products as a starting point from which to discuss current events and trends in their homeland. Interestingly, she further added that she feels a little more Korean when consuming and talking about Korean cultural products with her co-ethnics because they restore her connection with her ethnic identity, a connection that has somewhat eroded since her immigration. She therefore sees her engagement with Facebook not just as a means to socialize with her co-ethnics, but also as a bridge connecting her to her ethnic identity. In other words, Facebook is more than a technological means to connect with co-ethnics on a surface level, but a deep, virtual playground that allows one to continuously shape, reshape, and share his or her ethnic identity while staking claims to the cultures of which he or she is a part through the information they choose to share (Wardyga, 2012).

One last example among first-and-a-half generation interviewees for the purposes of this analysis is David (17, M, Rural), whose life in the U.S. is still very connected to his parents and friends, who are currently living in Korea, via intensive engagement over KakaoTalk (as shown in Figure 3.8 (see Chapter Three)). To investigate his views of his ethnic identity, the interviewer asked, "So, what nationality or ethnicity do you consider yourself now?" He replied, "Um … I feel very Korean when I talk with my parents or friends on KakaoTalk because that is the only time I can communicate solely in Korean, without using any English at all." As Lee (2006) argues, language usage is not just an essential part of one's identity; it is a primary indicator of one's ethnic identity. In this context, then, David associates his maintenance and frequent use of the Korean language as a beacon of his Koreanness.

For David, maintaining his Korean language proficiency primarily derives from KakaoTalk chats with his parents and friends in Korea, but he supports that activity with Korean media consumption. This includes following Korean news stories as well as keeping up to date with K-pop, movies, and TV dramas using his digital media devices. Together, these activities help sustain his Korean language proficiency, but they simultaneously influence his ethnic identity in that he stays intimately connected to Korean culture while he is living in the U.S. It is digital media that allow for the various connections he has to his culture of origin, revealing how such technology plays a pivotal role in the interplay between the maintenance of a native language and the formation of an ethnic identity.

Interestingly, he added,

> I am a Korean … But, unlike my parents or friends back in Korea, I am a Korean who is also familiar with American culture because I feel very American when I hang out with my American friends. I guess that I feel very Korean or very American depending on the circumstances.

Although he initially claimed a Korean identity, he seems to differentiate himself from those born and raised exclusively in Korea because despite being Korean-born, he has received an American-style education and has been raised under the direct influence of American culture. He sees himself both as a Korean who is fluent in American culture and an American who is fluent in Korean culture, which fits the definition of a "Korean American."

When questioned further on the moments during which he feels more Korean or more American, he answered,

> I feel the same emotions my parents feel when I hear news about South Korea, such as South Korea-North Korea tensions over the North's nuclear missile tests and South Korea-Japan tensions over the Dokdo Islands or the comfort women issue … Those are the moments I feel very Korean. But, I also grow more concerned about increasing terrorism, especially after the September 11, 2001 attacks in America, when I watch news about terrorism on TV because I am now living in the U.S. I feel very American when my concerns for the future of America grow more and more …

David exists simultaneously in two different cultures, and, as such, his self-identity does not fit neatly into one particular box. Interpreted differently, his description of his identity reflects the high degree of flexible control that he exercises over the development of the Korean and American parts of his identity.

When he was asked if he plans to go back to Korea or stay in America after his high school graduation, he stressed,

> I plan to stay and work in America, to attend college and get a job after graduation. Whenever my American friends and I go out for breakfast at McDonald's, I place my own order instead of relying on them even though they are native-English speakers. Also, in Korean culture it's common for the most senior or oldest person in a group

> to pay the bill at a restaurant, but I go Dutch when I hang out with my American friends. I even try to learn about lots of different parts of American culture by taking my car to American rather than Korean mechanics because I enjoy talking with them and learning the various terms for car parts in English.

He appears to have a good impression of American culture and practices it in his everyday life. In this context, ordering breakfast at McDonald's, going Dutch at a restaurant, and taking his car to American mechanics, while ordinary activities in the quotidian sense, both demonstrate the degree of his cultural adaptation and act as a sign of acculturation.

When asked further, "How do your parents feel about your plan to stay in America in the future," he said, "My parents definitely want me to return to Korea after my college years. But, I believe I will enjoy staying here more." What seems striking about his decision is that he plans to do so despite his parents' wishes. His decision reflects a surprising degree of independence, which is not a common trait among native Korean-born and Korean-raised teenagers, who typically adhere to and obey the desires of their parents. He seems to have learned to appreciate the values of individuality and privacy associated with the American lifestyle. Therefore, the overall picture that David paints is of a boy who is at times more Korean than American and vice versa because he views both cultures simultaneously through the eyes of an outsider, a characteristic that was noticed in the other first-and-a-half generation interviewees as well.

Parallel to Suji's, Mari's, and David's cases, eight other first-and-a-half generation interviewees except Ha Sun, who claims a Korean identity, refuse to choose one identity at the expense of the other, choosing instead to identify themselves as "Korean Americans." Each one seems to demonstrate flexibility in switching back-and-forth between their Korean and American identities depending on with whom they socialize and the particular circumstance in which that socialization occurs. As such, each was asked if their digital media practices were influential in their self-identification as "Korean American," and the following interview excerpts illustrate the diverse ways in which digital media practices did in fact impact their ethnic identity.

Rose (17, F, Rural), who maintains solid ties with her friends in Korea via KakaoTalk despite residing in the U.S. (as shown in Figure 3.7 (see Chapter Three)), said,

> Without KakaoTalking, I won't be able to connect with my friends back home, and if they were not a part of my everyday life as they are now, I would feel less Korean. It's like my friends back home make up the Korean half of my Korean American identity.

Similarly, Min Joon (15, M, Metro), who has both American and Korean songs on his iPod (as shown in Figure 6.3 (see Chapter Six)), stated,

> K-pop is becoming more popular in Europe and even America, so Korea's overall reputation and the importance of the Korean language have grown. These positive changes have clearly had a huge impact on my Korean pride. I am very proud to be a Korean American. With the flexibility of my iPod, I can access any K-pop or its music video. K-pop is a part of my identity.

Likewise, Yoongi (17, M, City), who watches both American and Korean TV shows using his tablet, stressed,

> Popular Korean dramas or movies are always common things I talk about with my Korean American group of friends. Using YouTube to stay up-to-date on Korean entertainment is the best way for me to stay an active member of my group. Without it, I would be less aware … Then, I would feel left out.

The above set of responses demonstrates how these interviewees' digital media practices play a key role in their ethnic identity formation. While some first-and-a-half generation interviewees felt lost during their initial adaptation period and thus intensively engaged with their homeland, others felt an urge to adapt to their new environment because of that very same sense of loss. They went in a different direction, reporting an intentional disengagement with their homeland in order to more quickly learn English and adapt to American culture. However, even those who initially broke with their homeland reported that they eventually reengaged when they felt more comfortable in their host culture. While they certainly undergo re-socialization when coming to America, where they are introduced to and subsequently incorporate into their own identity the values, norms, and beliefs of American society, they still immerse themselves in various characteristics of Korean culture to carve out a comfortable enclave in which they can remain tied to their ethnic identity. Since digital media devices provide them with a variety of tools with which to remain in constant contact with their home country, all 12 first-and-a-half generation interviewees, whose lives were physically and socially upended as a result of relocating to the U.S., placed great importance on digital media as they both fueled and enabled their desire to incorporate Korean cultural elements into and even extend their ethnic identities in increasingly unique and significant ways.

## Ethnic Identity Development Among Second Generation Interviewees

At the beginning of the interview, the first impression of Eddie (16, M, Metro), who described his identity struggle using the compelling metaphor of a red fish swimming against the group (as shown in Figure 5.1), was of someone who is somewhat stoic and reserved. However, as the interview progressed, he began to open up and talk more about his identity struggle. During the interview, he mostly spoke English, but he naturally mixed in short Korean phrases, showing great pride in his ability to switch between the two languages as necessary. When he had the chance to speak Korean during the interview, he took it and was able to actively participate in that way with no misunderstandings. Eddie's primary language is English, but using his ethnic language alongside his regular use of English poses no problems for him.

As Eddie explained in his interview, he lives with his parents and his younger sister in a predominantly racial minority community in an urban area in California. His parents migrated from Korea to the U.S. several years before he was born. He is American-born and American-raised, fully equipped with the English language and a fluency in American culture, but his family speaks primarily Korean at home, eats Korean food, attends a local Korean church, and participates in traditional Korean holiday celebrations. So, he clearly perceives distinct differences between his home culture and American culture-at-large. Growing up as an American and attending school, he also perceives contradictions in his American identity in terms of his physical appearance compared to his American friends. While living between two different cultures, the forces of which are pulling him in different directions, he seems to experience the sense of being different both from his parents and his local peers because of the simple fact that he was born to Korean immigrants on American soil, as if he was born into and eventually became aware of two different cultures simultaneously. At the same time, he recognizes the continuous negotiation and balance that are required to manage the complexities and potential conflicts that may arise between his parents' culture of origin and the American social context in which he lives.

In terms of ethnic identity, he shared with the interviewer his view of himself, explaining how his identity is negotiated differently depending on the social context.

> I have two different groups of friends. I have school friends and church friends. School friends are all Americans. I mean that they are really Americans. I think I get along

> with all of them. And, my church friends are all like me. I feel more American when I am with my school friends. But, I feel more Korean when I am with my church friends.

Like most of the interviewees in this study, he seems to have two different social networks of friends: friends who are predominantly white Americans and friends who are co-ethnics with similar Korean cultural backgrounds.

Regarding his own view of his identity, he continued,

> I strongly believed that I was an American when I was young … But, when Americans looked at me, I realized that their first impression is that I am not one of them. Although I was born in the U.S., my parents originally came from Korea. Because my physical appearance and skin color are different from my American friends, it forms a kind of invisible wall between us in some aspects. For example, when one of them makes some kind of racial joke, others just laugh and laugh. But, I cannot laugh with them because I'm the child of immigrants and more familiar with how my parents experience life as a racial minority in the U.S. I don't mind hanging out with them … But, it hurts me when they make those jokes.

Most of the time, he does not seem to experience problems when hanging out with his American friends, but at certain moments when tensions arise, he takes note of the cultural differences between them and himself. What is further surprising here is how Eddie directly took on his parents' difficulties as immigrants in the U.S. as his own, which is indicative of the collectivist mentality typical of a Korean cultural identity.

To explain further, Eddie's quote reveals an interesting aspect of how he and other second generation interviewees internalize the struggles faced by their immigrant parents of living and working as minorities in the U.S. So, while not all second generation interviewees found it difficult to adopt American cultures, values, norms, and beliefs themselves, many still perceived and acutely empathized with their parents' struggles to do so. This collectivist family dynamic appears to influence how these youths view their own ethnic identities. Furthermore, it reflects the extreme importance of parents in their lives, which then speaks to one of the fundamental difference between Korean and American cultures as discussed in literature—that of filial piety-centered Confucian collectivism versus independence-centered American individualism (Hurh, 1998).

Regarding the racial jokes made by Eddie's friends, he was then asked whether he confronted them about his feelings. He replied,

> I felt uncomfortable … But, how would it be possible for them to understand my feelings when they make such jokes when they are white, are considered normal, and have never experienced racial discrimination? So, I bottled up my emotions and

> showed a tough and cool exterior because we are in the same classroom at the same school. I'm going to see them every day. There is not a single corner in my school where I can isolate myself from my American friends. We are in the same boat, in the same grade, and we will graduate together in the same year ...

He expressed frustration with his American friends more than once throughout the interview, but, at the same time, he expressed a simultaneous desire to be a member of that mainstream segment of American society in the future. Not only does he perceive differences between himself and his American friends physically and culturally, then, but he also understands that he must keep up with them as well as American cultures and norms if he is to see himself as an ordinary American citizen sans differences. This contradiction explains his mixed feelings about his identity.

Further discussion with Eddie revealed the critical moment that motivated him to explore his ethnic identity—a group conversation over KakaoTalk in which he was introduced to Girls' Generation, a Korean female group that became sensationally popular in Korea and have held concerts around the world. "When I first listened to Girls' Generation's song 'Gee,' it was a different experience for me, and I immediately became one of their fans," he said. K-pop was very appealing because it represented a part of his parents' original culture, but, for Eddie, its importance went beyond that. Listening to this catchy pop song from Girls' Generation over KakaoTalk marked the beginning of his desire to explore and engage with his cultural heritage. Thus, while he attributed this desire to encountering K-pop, he said that he became truly invested in exploring his ethnic identity as a result of subsequent discussions about Girls' Generation with his co-ethnic friends.

Learning more about K-pop in turn exposed him to other facets of Korean culture. Soon, he and his co-ethnic friends began talking about their ethnic identities in the context of Korean popular culture. He said,

> During the discussion, I found out that two members of this group, Jessica and Tiffany, are Korean Americans who are fluent in both English and Korean ... As Girls' Generation became popular around the world because of their music videos on YouTube, we, as a group, often watched them together and shared our thoughts on Facebook about how their successes around the world made us really proud of our Korean heritage. For me, learning about Jessica and Tiffany's stories in particular was the turning point that gave me a sense of pride as a Korean American.

His quote highlights two significant aspects of digital media technology: it is a means of cultural contact in which he can engage with his parents' culture as well as a cultural learning platform allowing him to explore what it means for himself to be a Korean American—one who possesses the cultural values and perspectives both of his parents and of America.

When asked, "So, what nationality or ethnicity do you consider yourself now? How does the cultural exposure through the digital media you engaged in influence your views about your identity," he answered,

> It's hard to say one term that I prefer. I don't think of myself as uni-cultural, but as a mixture of different cultures … I feel as if there are two different cultural identities inside me that split apart and come together depending on the needs of the moment. Listening to K-pop as a product of Korean culture and learning about Jessica and Tiffany's stories as Korean Americans has led me to believe that I don't need to claim one identity as if I'm ignoring the other. So, I feel that I am half Korean and half American because I was born here, but I'm a Korean by blood.

Fully aware of his distinctive physical appearance and with a better understanding of Korean culture, he prefers to be identified as a Korean American. He may identify more with one culture depending on the particular context of the moment, but the overall picture that he describes is of a cultural synthesis, a harmonious coexistence of two different cultural elements within his overall ethnic identity and a trait that was also readily apparent in other second generation interviewees.

For Eddie, Jessica and Tiffany's global success as Korean Americans seems to serve as a sort of map for his own life, revealing an alternative path to linearly adapting to mainstream society. More importantly, the catalyst for his nuanced thinking about his identity was his engagement with digital media. Were it not for digital media, which introduced him to the music that would then inform him about Korean culture and allay any concerns about his Korean identity, he may otherwise have rejected any Koreanness due to assimilation pressures. Indeed, at the end of the interview, when asked whether he would have experienced his identity transformation if digital media technology had been unavailable, he said that without such technology, he would not have been exposed to Korean popular culture or been able to consume it to the extent that he is doing now, thereby making him less certain of his ethnic identity. Eddie's case perfectly illustrates the sophisticated ways in which his digital media practices of exploring, consuming, and discussing Korean cultural content interweave to inform his ethnic identity negotiation processes as a Korean American in the U.S.

With respect to her ethnic identity and associated online behaviors, Jieun (17, F, City) explained, "I used to feel like I am living a double life because everything I did in the past was about following certain cultural and social rules." Her comment is indicative of her confusion and frustration at some point in her life regarding the pressure to follow the crowd. According to her, during her early childhood, because of the possible social consequences of interacting with co-ethnic friends, she felt that she did not belong with co-ethnic groups at school and naturally integrated into a group of all-white friends. While at her boarding school, away from her family, she began to feel a sense of honorary whiteness; she felt accepted by her white friends and was "just like them" because they regarded her as white or "un-Asian." A white friend told her that she perceived her to be white, which made her feel "accepted, I guess." Along with her comments, she showed a picture of her with her non-Korean friends. (see Figure 5.5)

She continued, "These are my closest friends from school. We do fight a lot and have stupid arguments over nothing, but in the end, we're always friends. We have the most fun times. I love them so much." She seems to be well integrated into the dominant American culture. However, she added one more comment: "Most of my friends are white … But, internally, I feel very, very Korean …" A few years ago, she started to recognize in certain ways that she was not white, including in her looks and life values. At the same time, she came to realize that her whiteness was an act and that she was unable to escape the sense of feeling forever foreign. To counteract this feeling, she turned to Facebook as a way to reconnect with her co-ethnic peers.

In describing one relationship with a co-ethnic friend that has developed over the years, she said, "This is one of my best friends. Her name is Karis. We first connected with each other on Facebook." (see Figure 5.6)

Jieun explained that she learned about Karis by reading her Facebook profile, which lists her favorite music, books, dramas, and movies. While browsing her Facebook profile and wall posts, she noticed a multitude of Korean cultural influences, eventually finding Karis' favorite Korean entertainment very appealing. By clicking the links that Karis posted on Facebook to her favorite content, Jieun was introduced to numerous Korean celebrities, movie and drama titles, and bands that she may never have known about otherwise. More than simply consuming content, though, she further described how she and Karis actively use Korean popular culture as a starting point for discussions about everything from Korean celebrity gossip to their individual ethnic identities. She added, "Since I met Karis online, learning about Korean popular culture has helped me get in touch with my ethnic identity more." Facebook is not only a useful platform on which Jieun can bond with her co-ethnic friend,

Karis, but it is also a highly dynamic and interactive space where she had her first meaningful contact with Korean popular culture and began exploring her own cultural heritage simply by browsing her friend's profile page.

It was Jieun's discussion of her two photos—one with her non-Korean friends and one with her best Korean friend—that provided a glimpse into the complexities of her bi-cultural social circles and raised provocative questions about her ethnic identity. She seems to regret that she spent much of her early childhood rejecting the Korean side of her identity. To rectify the situation, she is now trying to "get it back" by increasing the time she spends chatting with Karis via Facebook. She reported, "Karis speaks Korean fairly well and types Korean pretty well … I wish my Korean fluency can be as good as hers. I am now trying to learn more Korean by watching Korean dramas on YouTube." For her, familiarity with Korean popular culture goes hand-in-hand with her ethnic identity since the former reflects an increased understanding of Korean culture and the Korean language, which she considers important to her Korean identity. Therefore, socialization and the consumption of Korean popular culture, which simultaneously occur in the particular context of Facebook, combine to function as a source of motivation for her to both learn her ethnic language and preserve her ethnic identity.

When treated like an honorary white in the past, Jieun took to distancing herself from her co-ethnic group and claiming herself as "American." However, at the time of the interview, she considered Karis to be her best friend and Korean popular culture to be a source of ethnic pride, the latter especially making her proud to call herself a "Korean American." Her newfound claim is a marked contrast with her earlier childhood description of her tendency to reject her Koreanness. As she explains it, corresponding with Karis online has totally changed her perception of being a Korean American, particularly in terms of her newfound access to her Korean cultural heritage. Whereas with her non-Korean friends she rejected her Korean identity, her socialization with Karis seems to have provided Jieun with both the space and support she needs to fully negotiate her own ethnic identity without worrying whether or not she is adhering to the mainstream white culture of her non-Korean friends.

Jieun further expressed her determination to maintain her uniqueness as a Korean American, but she also emphasized her desire to continue hanging out with her non-Korean friends at school. When discussing her own Facebook page, she reported that she now carefully balances the content she shares so that it does not imply a bias toward either Korean or American culture. By using Facebook in this way, she is able to present her dual identities—one that speaks to her relationship with her non-Korean friends, where she adheres closely to mainstream American culture, and another in the context of her co-ethnic friends, where she appears comfortable being who she is. This multifaceted relationship she has with Facebook shows how the site is uniquely suited to help her define, explore, and express her ethnic identity in ways that balance the cultures of which she is a part.

Jieun is not alone in how she sees herself as a Korean American. Ivy (17, F, Metro) also expressed feeling both like an honorary white and a forever foreigner at various times as well as on one particular occasion. She shared with the interviewer the following pictures, which were posted on her Instagram page as her favorite photos. "I chose these pictures because my friends make me who I am and understand me in all that I do," she said. (see Figure 5.7)

Ivy took several pictures of her senior banquet, where she and her co-ethnic friends celebrated their upcoming high school graduation. The collage of four pictures above, just a few of the many she took at that event, is meant to show how these special friends are always there to support her in the event of racial insecurities or incidences of stereotyping by sharing their own, similar experiences as immigrant children to furnish her with a sense of belonging.

In terms of socializing, Ivy corresponds frequently with her co-ethnic friends using KakaoTalk to share her struggles and the emotions she is feeling.

> Being different from my White American friends means that I sometimes come face-to-face with white supremacy or white privilege … Those things really bother me … When I feel down because of some conflicts I have with my American friends, we [Ivy and her co-ethnic friends] assure one another that we are all in the same boat. These interactions are what make my Korean identity stronger, and they make me feel a little more in touch with my Koreanness.

Ivy and her friends' ethnic interactions using KakaoTalk seem to transform their distinctive cultural heritage into a kind of ethnic armor, allowing them to establish a sense of collective dignity that enables them to cope psychologically, even in the face of prejudice and discrimination.

When discussing her emerging interest in her ethnic background, Ivy described the guilt she used to feel when non-Korean friends asked her about the tension between North and South Korea and her not being able to answer them because of her lack of knowledge about the issue. She used this past example of her ignorance of her Korean cultural roots as evidence of being formerly disconnected from her Koreanness. She further felt that non-Korean friends unfamiliar with North and South Korea often misinterpret news reports about tensions between the two countries, pointing out their inability to distinguish between North and South Koreans portrayed in movies as a sign of their lack of perception. Indeed, she became truly engaged in exploring her ethnic background in part because of her desire to demonstrate to her non-Korean friends that their views about North and South Korea are based on misconceptions and prejudice. She reported that before her non-Korean friends came to her with these questions, she had been dabbling in Korean culture, but that the questions spurred her to look more into Korean history, culture, and traditions.

Ivy particularly relied on Google and YouTube to begin an investigation into North and South Korea and gather details about their cultures. As she reported, this multipronged investigation elicited numerous texts for her to study, including pictures of various locations and K-pop, Korean dramas, and Korean movies. At the same time, it gave her access to viewpoints not found in her American school curriculum or even in American news media, viewpoints which were key to her ethnic identity construction. Furthermore, in this investigation of Korean culture, she began to perceive aspects of her own ethnic identity that she had previously overlooked and found new ways to relate to her ethnic heritage. She said that her online search convinced her that her ethnic identity should play a larger role in her life than it had up to that point. At the time of the interview, she claimed that she expressed greater comfort with her ethnic identity, therefore choosing to identify herself as a Korean American and expressing a desire to balance both her Korean and American identities.

As evidence of her connection with her ethnic identity, she said, "I feel like what you post on Facebook for others to see is what matters to you, in a sense. These pictures of my friends and me at the senior banquet are showing who I am becoming." In this quote, she seems to feel that her co-ethnic friends are a significant component of her ethnic identity, and that by uploading the pictures for all to see, she is inviting others to know about her through those pictures.

When asked what specifically makes her feel Korean, she stressed,

> When non-Korean school friends show an interest in Korea or Korean culture, I'm no longer afraid to talk about it. I felt proud when they appreciated the information I gave them about Korea and K-pop. Now, I am the one who gets to show off my cultural heritage in front of everyone else.

An important point in this quote, which Ivy emphasized, is how her investigation not only reinforced her ties with her ethnic identity, but also helped her defend her cultural heritage against misconceptions or provide an important counterpoint to stereotypes about North and South Korea. For her, this newfound familiarity with Korea and its culture is a marker that shows how connected she is to her ethnic identity.

As is evident from her quotes, Ivy's ethnic identity construction is strongly influenced by her digital media practice. When asked if she thinks that digital media play a role in keeping her ethnic identity alive, she said,

> If I didn't have digital media, I wouldn't be able to strike out on my own to explore my cultural origins and ethnic identity … Using digital media, I was able to build on what I already knew about Korea and my Korean identity with the information I got from multiple searches … Moreover, Facebook became a space of my own where I can express my Korean identity in many different ways.

Ivy seems to attribute her newfound ethnic identity to her routine digital media practice and the technology itself, without which she would not be able to flexibly express her ethnic identity or even retain it.

Furthermore, Ivy was critical of those peers who she feels are losing touch with their ethnic identity by not taking advantage of the diverse digital media technology to which they all have access. She stated, "In the world we live in today, with all the technology available to us, I believe that anyone can learn about Korea and its culture if they're just willing to do some simple searches." Ivy believes that other Korean American teenagers in addition to herself should explore their original culture and ethnic identity using digital media technology not only for the sake of their individual identity, but as a way to competently inform non-Koreans who inquire about or are interested in Korea and its culture. Her exuberance regarding this issue reflects the appeal of digital media technology, which for her serves a key role in ethnic identity exploration and expression. Compared with other interviewees who did not engage in direct exploration of Korea, Korean culture, and Korean social and political issues using digital media technology, but instead focused on Korean popular culture as a proxy, Ivy is a notable exception. Thus, her particular case highlights the transformational power of digital media technology in that her online investigation of Korea and Korean culture evolved into a critical exploration of her own ethnic identity and how that identity would become an integral part of her life.

Many second generation interviewees oscillate between American and Korean identities in their everyday lives, and just one more example of this phenomenon is John (15, M, Metro). He showed three photos that demonstrate his comfort both in a local American soccer team and as a part of a group of friends defined by their common Korean ancestry. He said, "I am a soccer player in a club at my school. I started to play when I was five or six years old. In the future, I want to be a professional soccer player." In sharing this picture, he seems proud to have been picked as a member of his local soccer team, which is dominated by very competitive and mostly white American soccer players. (see Figure 5.8)

John continued,

> Because I want to be a professional soccer player, I often look at highlights of soccer games or players on YouTube. I try to understand what they do on the field and see how well they play together as a team. My role models for soccer are Ji Sung Park and Christiano Ronaldo. In particular, I am a really big fan of Ji Sung Park. He is my soccer hero because he carries the pride of the Korean people with him. I put his picture on my Facebook page so that my friends can look at him and know who he is. Actually, he is a very popular figure among my friends because he is a very well-known professional soccer player.

Even though John plays soccer as an American at an American high school, rather than idolize an American soccer star as his teammates might, his role model is Ji Sung Park, a Korean soccer hero who is recognized as one of the best soccer players on the world stage.

John used his idolization of an iconic Korean soccer star as evidence of his connection with and pride in his Korean roots. In discussing his notion of Korean pride, he candidly shared the following anecdote.

> One of the common interests that I talk about with others online is sports, for example soccer. When the London Summer Olympics were held in 2012, my Korean friends and I showed our strong support for the Korean national team. Cheers for Korea's national soccer team by the Red Devils cheering squad really stood out during the tournament, so we also wore "Be the Reds!" t-shirts and gathered in my home to watch and root for the Korean national soccer team on satellite television. The Korean team's victory over Great Britain in a penalty shootout was the most unforgettable moment for all of us. I felt that this occasion collectively made us all extremely proud to be Korean.

From his quotes, not movies or music, as with other interviewees, but an international and intercultural sporting event—the Olympics—was the catalyst for his immense pride in his ethnic identity. Indeed, his Koreanness was palpable when he told of his strong support for the Korean national soccer team during the interview.

At the end of the interview, as an example of his willingness to express his ethnic identity on Facebook, John showed the following picture and said,

> After watching and cheering together for the Korean team during each game, we frequently shared our thoughts and comments on KakaoTalk and on our Facebook pages. This is the Korean flag, which proudly represents my parents' homeland. I decorated my Facebook page with this Korean national flag soon after the Korean team's victory against Great Britain at the Olympics. I was born and raised here, but at that moment of victory, I definitely felt honored to carry on my parents' original cultural heritage. (see Figure 5.9)

John was bold enough to express his ethnic identity on the world of Facebook. When asked about other friends' reactions to his posting a Korean flag on his Facebook page, he said, "The post with the Korean flag picture had more than 20 positive comments in a mix of Korean and English …" It appears from his peers' reactions, then, that their overwhelming show of support indicates their acceptance of his choice to publicly showcase his ethnic identity by virtually flying the Korean flag. He described the positive responses he received, both from Korean American and non-Korean friends, as motivation to continue to foreground his ethnic identity. When asked further, "Aren't you afraid that expressing your ethnic identity too visibly on Facebook might make other friends perceive you as being too ethnocentric," he stressed, "No, I am not … I am not hesitant to express my ethnic identity both on and off Facebook … When my friends see my Facebook page, I want to make sure that the page reflects who I am." Bolstering this quote further, he added that friends who are unsupportive of his public commitment to his ethnic identity are not truly considered friends. For John, then, any possible negative social consequences were not major deterrents to his foregrounding his ethnic identity, not only in the virtual world of Facebook but also in the real world.

When asked, "In the event of a match between the Korean and American national soccer teams in the coming Olympic games or the World Cup, which team would you support," John paused for a moment and said,

> Usually, when the American national soccer team is up against any other team than Korea in world sporting events, I will show my strong support for them. But, I am sure that I will cheer and show my support for the Korean national team because I believe my parents would cheer for the Korean national soccer team, too.

Of interest here is John's prefacing his response by stating how his parents would do the same. This seems to imply parental pressure to cheer for the Korean national team, but the reality is more complicated in that his support for either team is not dependent on whether he is watching a game with his parents or his American friends but is a sign of his bi-cultural flexibility. He cheers for Korea because of his strong ethnic pride. After all, his role model is Korean soccer star Ji Sung Park. He also roots for the American team because he is an American high school soccer player. However, he would support Korea over America not because of pressure from his parents, but for the same reason that they would—collective pride in the accomplishments of the Korean team. John's support is out of respect for his parents' culture and therefore related to his ethnic orientation and enthusiastic adherence to his ethnic identity.

In John's case, his online behavior, including posting pictures of Ji Sung Park and the Korean national flag on his Facebook page, is directly tied to his pride in his ethnic heritage and his desire to visibly manifest his ethnic identity. In terms of that identity, although he enthusiastically adhered to his Koreanness, he rejects fixed cultural boundaries in favor of openness to cultural flux and change; therefore, he considers himself to be a Korean American. When asked, "What does it mean to you to be a Korean American," he answered,

> I find that I sometimes really identify with my Korean side. Other times, however, I identify with my American side. So, I somehow try to blend each side [Korean or American] together into a complete idea of "me." In the end, I feel that having two cultures inside me is very special.

John's explanations show that he is simultaneously holding open bi-cultural identities, so he is clearly demonstrating a more fluid understanding of his own ethnic identity.

Consistent with Eddie's, Jieun's, Ivy's, and John's cases, 15 other second generation interviewees passionately refuse to label themselves primarily as American or Korean, choosing instead to refer to themselves as Korean Americans. When each was asked if their digital media practices were influential in their self-identification as "Korean American," the one commonality that permeated their descriptions of their media landscape as it relates to their Korean identities was the consumption of Korean popular culture (K-pop, TV dramas, entertainment shows, movies, etc.) using their digital media devices. This includes everything from individually searching for Korean songs on YouTube to sharing and discussing content in group chats on KakaoTalk. While some interviewees see their relationship with Korean popular culture as a frankly enjoyable way to practice and improve their Korean language skills, others use the knowledge gained from the content they consume—knowledge including celebrities' personal stories to Korean historical data—to instead support their passionate claims to their ethnic identity.

Although second generation interviewees are positioned between two conflicting cultural forces, they do not appear to be metaphorically stuck in that they must choose one culture at the expense of the other. In contrast, they all seem capable of observing both cultures in-depth and subsequently selecting those aspects with which they are most comfortable and which speak to their most closely held beliefs, values, and attitudes that form their core identity. More importantly, all 19 second generation interviewees emphasized from their own unique perspectives the importance of digital media in negotiating how where they came from impacts their place in their social worlds as media both enabled and fueled their desire to weave their cultural spheres together into more flexible bi-cultural identities. Thus, the core takeaway from the interviewees' responses regarding their digital media usage is that diverse media texts and technologies have become enmeshed in their daily lives to the point that they are not only highly influential, but indeed inseparable parts of their ethnic identities.

## References

Akhtar, S. (2011). *Immigration and acculturation: Mourning, adaptation, and the next generation.* Lanham, MD: Jason Aronson.

Elias, N., & Lemish, D. (2008). The Internet life of Former Soviet Union adolescents in Israel. In I. Rydin & U. Sjöberg (Eds.), *Mediated crossroads: Identity, youth culture and ethnicity—Theoretical and methodological challenges* (pp. 173–192). Göteborg, Sweden: Nordicom, Göteborg University.

Fogt, A., & Sandvik, M. (2008). We represent a potential, not a problem: Young people's media use in diaspora. *Nordicom Review, 29*(1), 111–131.

Hurh, W. M. (1998). *The Korean Americans*. Westport, CT: Greenwood Press.

Lee, J. S. (2006). Exploring the relationship between electronic literacy and heritage language maintenance. *Language Learning and Technology*, *10*(2), 93–113.

Lee, R. M. (2003). Do ethnic identity and other-group orientation protect against discrimination for Asian Americans? *Journal of Counseling Psychology*, *50*, 133–141.

Livingstone, S. (2008). Internet literacy: Young people's negotiation of new online opportunities. In T. McPherson (Ed.), *Digital youth, innovation, and the unexpected* (pp. 101–122). Cambridge: MIT Press.

Wardyga, B. J. (2012). *The relationship between text message volume and formal writing performance among upper level high school students and college freshmen.* (Doctoral dissertation). Retrieved from http://digitalcommons.liberty.edu/cgi/viewcontent.cgi?article=1577&context=doctoral

Figure 5.1. The Red Fish.
Source: Photo by Eddie.

Figure 5.2. Map of Korea.
Source: Photo by Ha Sun.

Figure 5.3. *Potbingsoo*, a Korean Popular Dessert.
Source: Photo by Suji.

Figure 5.4. My Pencil Cases Made in Korea.
Source: Photo by Mari.

Figure 5.5. My Non-Korean Friends at School.
Source: Photo by Jieun.

Figure 5.6. With My Best Friend.
Source: Photo by Jieun.

Figure 5.7. Senior Banquet.
Source: Photo by Ivy.

Figure 5.8. My Play at the Soccer Field.
Source: Photo by John.

Figure 5.9. Korean Flag.
Source: Photo by John.

· 6 ·

# DIGITAL MEDIA BILINGUALISM

The discussion of identity formation and digital media would not be complete without reference to the role of bilingualism in the lives of first-and-a-half and second generation Korean American youths. Surprisingly, what becomes clear in interviews with these teens is their simultaneous mastery of both English and Korean while preserving a cultural anchor in their family's past. Some of the interviewees in this study claimed that their use of Korean is a particularly powerful vehicle for expressing their most personal thoughts and feelings, and a good majority made it quite clear that their regular use of English does not equate to diminished Korean language abilities.

## Bilingualism in the Interviews

Regarding this strong bilingual and bi-cultural orientation, David (17, M, Rural) showed a screenshot that he captured to help describe how he frequently alternates back-and-forth between English and Korean to communicate with different groups of friends. As discussed previously, and as shown in Figure 3.8 (see Chapter Three) David communicates extensively with his parents, who are currently living in Korea, via KakaoTalk, and he does so exclusively in Korean. As a point of departure from his dialogue with his parents, the screenshot below is taken from actual exchanges between David and his friend, the former being Korean American and the latter being American. (see Figure 6.1)

In the screenshot, his Korean American friend's screen name is written in Korean, and there is a plentiful blending of English and Korean in the messages they exchange with each other. David explained why he prefers mixing Korean and English when he detailed the context and circumstances of his exchanges with his Korean American friend:

> I am now attending an American public school in the U.S., but I was born in Korea and grew up there until I was 12 years old. For me, Korean language and Korean culture are more important than English and American culture. So, I don't want to lose my Korean vocabulary.

Since he spent many of his formative years in Korea and thus has a deep-rooted personal connection to the country and culture, his concern about possibly losing his proficiency in his mother language seems very real, so he intentionally conducts most of his social interactions with co-ethnic groups of friends in Korean to preserve his proficiency.

When asked, "If your everyday language is English now, how do you keep up with sustaining Korean language proficiency," he replied,

> As I said before, much of my personal life revolves around KakaoTalk, so I connect with my parents and friends in Korea using only Korean. I believe that communicating only in Korean is a way to stay fluent and even improve my language skills ... Also, when I use regular text messages with my Korean American friends, I usually chat with them in Korean or a mixture of Korean and English. So, my regular use of English every day does not mean that I am losing any Korean language skills.

Even though David's living environment has physically and socially changed as a result of relocating to the U.S., he indeed seems reluctant to lose his Korean language proficiency. (see Figure 6.2)

In contrast to his first smartphone screenshot, his second one shows his American friend's screen name—written in English—as well as an English-only conversation. He reflected on his friendship with this American friend, saying,

> He is one of my best friends in the U.S. His parents invited me to join them on their family vacation last summer, so I went to Florida together with them. It was fun and very memorable. So, I don't talk or hang out only with my Korean friends.

Implied in David's response is that his level of English ability is not so large an obstacle that it impairs his social interactions with Americans. Indeed, after being immersed in an English-speaking environment for several years, he also finds it easier to express certain ideas or opinions in English, and the activities in which he chooses to participate are not so different from those of the majority of Americans. He is therefore in the center of mainstream American culture and certainly seems to engage in meaningful interactions with other Americans.

When asked further, "Has your digital media consumption changed since you immigrated, and, if so, how," David continued,

> Yes, I now watch American TV as part of my daily routine. But, as a source of Korean news updates, I usually visit the popular news website *Naver*. I also browse *USADISK*, a Korean site where users can watch many Korean dramas and entertainment programs. Using my smartphone, I watch Korean media like I eat Korean food here. It helps me to be knowledgeable about all the details of Korean daily life, such as famous celebrities and popular TV drama characters, so that I can join in Korean-language conversations with my parents and friends who are in Korea. This is the way I stay a part of my country, Korea.

Along with his daily conversations in Korean with his parents over KakaoTalk, his constant consumption of Korean media using his smartphone is yet another means by which he bolsters his Korean language proficiency so he can, as he said, stay a part of his country and culture.

David's varied efforts to preserve his Korean language proficiency as well as his reluctance to lose touch with his country and culture parallels the experiences of several other interviewees. A quote from Min Joon (15, M, Metro) also supports this observation.

> I use my iPod as an everyday portable music device. The moment I wake up, I put my earbuds in and turn on my iPod. Listening to music is like breathing to me. When I am back from school, I listen to music again. So, if I don't have music on, it's sort of weird. I listen to super popular American songs. But, I often listen to K-pop, too. (see Figure 6.3)

As can be seen in the photo, there was an eclectic mixture of American and Korean song titles on Min Joon's iPod. Not content with just listening, though, he also described the times that he sings Korean songs with his friend, usually when watching YouTube on-the-go via his smartphone. Based on the conversation with him, listening to K-pop comprises a significant part of his leisure activities. When asked, "What traits of K-pop do you single out as differing from traits of American music," Min Joon's answer was immediate:

> The best thing about K-pop is that most K-pop songs are not only fun and exciting, but also extremely catchy. The catchy, high-pitched tones easily get stuck in my head. Sometimes, they are also much more fun to dance to.

Although he does not understand every Korean word in each song, as he admitted, Min Joon can at least grasp the gist of each verse. By listening to K-pop via his iPod, then, he feels that he is brushing up on his Korean language skills. Actually, several other interviewees acknowledged following this same routine—using their smartphones to download and listen to the latest K-pop as recommended by their co-ethnic peers. They also further claimed that following K-pop serves dual functions in that they can surpass their co-ethnic friends (who may not follow K-pop as closely) in their knowledge of Korea and greatly improve their Korean listening and speaking proficiency.

In a similar fashion, Sun (15, M, Rural) showed an interesting picture as part of his response.

> This is me. My friends at school call me Pi because I am good at math. When Psy's "Gangnam Style" got really popular on YouTube, I sometimes said that Psy is my uncle, and they said like, "Really?" They believed that. So, sometimes they even call me Psy, too. Do I look like Psy? (see Figure 6.4)

Sun further discussed the indirect pressure he felt to listen to K-pop because of its popularity even with those outside of his ethnic community. When asked to clarify why he felt he should learn even more about K-pop, he answered,

> I think that Psy's music video is just so funny. That's why people like him and his song. It had one billion views on YouTube. [Rural] is just a small college town in the mid-west, but they even played it here on local radio stations … Even my American friends asked me what he's saying when they heard the song on the radio or watched the video on YouTube because they know that I'm from South Korea. So, I'd be embarrassed if I was not familiar enough with the song to explain each verse to them. Now, they know at least three Korean words in the melody of the song.

It seems that Sun's motivation for diving deeper into K-pop is based on a combination of guilt and pride: guilt when his lack of knowledge keeps him from participating in conversations about K-pop and pride when he is able to explain the meaning of Korean words and phrases to non-Koreans who express an interest in K-pop.

Interestingly, Sun was the only interviewee to describe in detail his intentional consumption of K-pop to prove his Korean language proficiency outside of his ethnic community. This is because he believes that outsiders who know he is a Korean and who are familiar with K-pop would expect him to have that same knowledge and more in addition to Korean language fluency. An important aspect of K-pop consumption for him, then, is that consumption is equivalent to language maintenance, allowing him to show his pride in his Korean language proficiency outside of his ethnic community.

Musical lyrics were not the only text that interviewees used to demonstrate their language proficiency. Two out of 31 interviewees instead showed photos of their own Bibles, both of which were Korean-English, as evidence of their simultaneous mastery of Korean and English even though the two interviewees were born in the U.S. One of the two interviewees was Jun Soo (16, M, Rural). The first time Jun Soo and the Korean speaking interviewer met, he greeted her by saying "Hi" in Korean and bowing. When she asked him a question in English, he usually responded in English, but when asked in Korean, he replied in Korean. The interviewer found it fascinating to watch an American-born and American-raised Korean American teenager speak in flawless, unaccented Korean.

Jun Soo placed a high importance on the picture of his Korean-English Bible to explain his extraordinary efforts to learn and achieve a high level of proficiency in Korean. According to him,

> I always take my Bible with me every time I go to my church. Reading my Bible is an important part of my Christian faith. Most of the time, I read my Bible in Korean even though my English-language reading ability is about the same. I believe that reading my Bible in Korean helps me remain in constant touch with the Korean language. (see Figure 6.5)

For Jun Soo, attending his Korean church on Sunday and reserving Friday nights for Bible study mean more than just practicing his religion. He explained that during Bible study, his youth group leader picks several verses from the Bible to use for discussion at meetings. While studying those verses, he uses *Naver* dictionary [an online Korean-English and English-Korean dictionary] on his smartphone to look up new words or translate from one language to the other, which introduces him to more advanced Korean vocabulary words and the necessary contextual information to better understand the verses in Korean. Yet, his Bible is Korean-English, meaning that he does not even need to read it in Korean if he can sufficiently understand the English version.

Nevertheless, the convenience of accessing the internet on his smartphone encourages him to focus on reading and understanding the Korean version, which has proven to be difficult but rewarding. Indeed, it seems that this kind of online engagement not only strengthens his Christian faith, but it also helps him maintain a better command of the Korean language.

When asked, "What got you started learning Korean in the first place," he showed another picture and said, "My friend took this picture to show that I am a hardworking Korean American boy. This is my classroom. I am checking my grade after my literature class final." (see Figure 6.6)

Pointing to himself in the picture, Jun Soo continued,

> The difference between the two cultures [American and Korean] that I can think of is education ... like, the value of education in each culture. My parents think education matters the most for me, which means getting good grades in high school and getting into a good college. But, while they of course want me to do well in school here in the U.S., they fear that they might lose me if I become too Americanized. So, with their support, I received both English and Korean language training. Every Saturday, I learn Korean at the Korean language school, which is supported by the Korean Embassy and held at the local Korean church … Also, my parents encourage me to watch Korean media so that they can discuss the content in Korean with me.

What is significant about this portion of his interview is how proactive his parents are regarding their concern for his Korean language acquisition, using Korean language school as a physical site of intense language education to complement their exposing him to Korean media in order to maintain his Korean language proficiency. Based on the set of responses from interviewees, several parents seem to have sent their second generation children to Korea for educational and cultural programs, including summer language school. Although they find visiting Korea from the U.S. both expensive and time-consuming, when it comes to sending their own children, they appear to be more than willing to cover the costs of both the round-trip tickets and the programs themselves given the perceived benefits for their children, specifically learning Korean and internalizing a sense of ethnic pride. In fact, some interviewees said that they were able to identify more strongly with their Korean heritage and use the Korean language more fluently with their families and co-ethnic friends after attending such language and cultural programs in Korea.

When asked, "Then, what is your daily consumption of digital media like," he spoke further of the impact that his digital media practice has on his Korean language proficiency.

> Using my tablet, I watch both American and Korean TV shows. For Korean TV shows, I go to several websites like *Drama Fever* and some free Korean websites. Most of the time, I understand Korean dramas without subtitles. So, on one hand, with my best Korean American friend, I talk about Korean TV programs I have watched over the weekend. On the other hand, I watch *Family Guy* and *The Simpsons* so that I can talk with my American friends who like those programs.

As his remarks show, he uses his tablet to consume both Korean and American media, activities which improve and solidify his language abilities as well as general cultural knowledge in that they allow him to more easily participate in broader discussions with his co-ethnic and American friends about popular TV programs.

Another American-born interviewee, Lana (17, F, Metro), also used a picture of her Korean-English Bible to represent her mastery of both languages. She asserted,

> I started to go to a Korean church because of my parents, but now I have become very active in my church and have a lot of knowledge about the Bible. This is my Bible, and when I read it, I read it in Korean. I am even able to listen to Korean-language audio recordings of the Bible online and understand most of what I hear. (see Figure 6.7)

During Lana's interview, she was able to express her complex thoughts and emotions in Korean, demonstrating a remarkably good command of the Korean language. According to her, just like Jun Soo, she learned Korean by attending an after-school Korean private supplementary institution in her neighborhood. However, the interviewer also found that Lana's parents strongly influenced her language acquisition by encouraging her to become a part of "Sunday culture" and watch TV programs with them, programs from their former homeland that research shows enhance family togetherness (Lemish, 2015, p. 153). She said, "As for American shows, I watch *Modern Family* and *New Girl*. As for Korean shows, I often watch Korean entertainment and variety programs, such as *Running Man* and *Infinity Challenge*, with my family every Sunday evening." For her, watching Korean media programs with her family is not just a way to spend time with them, but it is an explicitly cultural activity in which she can become immersed in and learn about her ethnic language.

The picture and her stories certainly speak to her Korean language proficiency, but they also tease out how she consumes Korean popular culture using digital media. She said,

> I mostly visit YouTube to listen to my favorite Korean popular artists, such as Girls' Generation and Super Junior. Girls' Generation and Super Junior are two of the top K-pop groups in Korea, and they have toured across the world. There are band members that can both sing and dance, but not all members are expected to be good in everything; instead, they have specific roles in the group, such as main vocalist, rapper, or dancer. When it comes to their dances, they are simply amazing. Their most eye-popping choreography includes hand-stands, backflips, splits, and popping. They are very precise and completely in sync. It is so addicting.

It appears that the more Lana is immersed in Korean through her increased consumption of Korean popular culture, the greater her interest in better understanding Korean culture and the Korean language becomes. This mirrors findings by Lee (2004), who described an interesting function of Korean television programming as helping to spark interest in learning Korean, especially among the second generation. While many interviewees seemed to agree on the value of the local Korean church as well as the summer language and cultural programs in Korea, both of which are integral to improving Korean language proficiency and strengthening ethnic pride, consuming K-pop culture through internet-capable smartphones was popular with this group due to their role in maintaining fluency in their Korean language. This desire to maintain proficiency in their mother language is at the forefront of their smartphone adoption and usage, subsequently impacting their Korean television viewing practices.

As revealed in the above examples, learning Korean as well as immersing oneself in Korean popular culture through the internet via smartphone or tablet is a distinctive characteristic of the lives of most of these tech-savvy interviewees. Although the degree of their Korean language proficiency may vary, they all emphasized from their differing perspectives the importance of the Korean language in their own lives. As Park's (2009) research suggests, the in-depth responses of the interviewees in this study provide evidence for a strong bilingualism among Korean American teens who are residing in the U.S., which is contrary to classical assimilation theory, where becoming American means losing one's ethnic language (Alba & Nee, 1997; Gordon, 1964; Park, 1928; Warner & Srole, 1945). More importantly with regards to their bilingualism, digital media technology that was already found to assist in relationship development and maintenance and ethnic media consumption now also seems to be playing a larger role in helping these teens to both foster and retain proficiency in their ethnic language.

## Bilingualism as Captured in Survey Data

According to Lee (2006), language usage is not just an essential part of one's identity; it is a primary indicator of one's ethnic identity. The survey therefore contained a question designed to determine if participants use the Korean language as opposed to English when they text (see Appendix B). In terms of generation status, among 154 participants, 28 participants (18.2%) are first-and-a-half generation and 126 participants (81.8%) are second generation, meaning that the vast majority of the participants in this study are second generation Korean Americans.

Much like through other forms of communication, personal writing styles, phraseology, and language use become habitualized through texting over time to form one's unique personal expressions, which then further become an important part of his or her identity. Note that of all participants, regardless of generation status, most use Korean when they engage in texting. Indeed, the results presented in Table 6.1 echo the bilingualism that was demonstrated by participants in the PEIs. Of those who text, the vast majority of first-and-a-half generation participants and three-quarters of second generation participants reported that they use Korean in addition to English in their messages. Of particular interest is that the second generation participants also show a strong bilingualism in their text messaging despite many of them being American-born and American-raised. Although the percentage who reported using Korean and English in their messages is less than that of the first-and-a-half generation (72.2% to the latter's 96.4%), 91 of 126 second generation participants who can and do use both languages is a significant number despite the disproportionately large pool of second generation participants in the survey sample (see Table 6.1). Furthermore, as research indicates that past second generations were in fact reluctant to learn or use Korean alongside their regular use of English in daily conversation, this unexpected result illuminates a newly emergent second generation firmly tethered to their homeland even while fully immersed in an American cultural environment. When combined, the survey data indicate that three-quarters (118 out of 154) of all participants (first-and-a-half and second generation) supplement their regular use of English with Korean when they engage in texting, demonstrating a desire to maintain an intimate connection with Korean culture even while living in the U.S. and adapting to American society.

As discussed previously during the PEI analyses, all first-and-a-half generation and second generation interviewees emphasized from their diverse and unique perspectives the importance of the Korean language in their own lives. Some further claimed that Korean was preferable and indeed more comfortable for expressing their most personal thoughts and feelings, and many described how they flexibly alternate between English and Korean to communicate with different groups of friends in their daily lives. In the past, supporters of the classical assimilation perspective argued that the nearly uncontested adoption of English as a common language was evidence of the contemporary second generation's linear pattern of assimilation into American society. However, the particular cases of these children of Korean immigrants in the U.S. do not support a scenario of a linear and universal adoption of the English language. Instead, as Park's (2009) research suggests, these children of Korean immigrants residing in the U.S. appear to follow a segmented assimilation model wherein their mastery of English does not come at the expense of their Korean (Song, 2003), as evinced both from their in-depth responses during PEIs and the results of survey data. From segmented assimilation theory's point of view, retention of one's ethnic language carries tremendous value as part of one's ethnic identity development.

Table 6.1. Usage of Korean Language Through Texting.

| | Generation Status | | |
|---|---|---|---|
| Usage of Korean Language | 1.5 (%) | 2nd (%) | Total (%) |
| Yes | 27 (96.4) | 91 (72.2) | 118 (76.6) |
| No | 1 (3.6) | 35 (27.8) | 36 (23.4) |
| Total | 28 (100) | 126 (100) | 154 (100) |

In addition, the survey contained a question designed to determine if participants often visit Korean, English, or both Korean and English websites when surfing the internet (see Appendix B). Interestingly, while none (0%) of the first-and-a-half generation participants reported that they often visit English websites, about a tenth of second generation participants reported that they often visit Korean websites (see Table 6.2). Among the participants, three-quarters of the first-and-a-half generation participants and half of the second generation participants reported that they do often visit both Korean and English websites. This suggests that more than half of the participants in this study are influenced by both Korean and English websites throughout their ethnic identity development process. This number is not particularly surprising with regards to first-and-a-half generation participants, who were born in Korea, spent at least some of their formative years in Korea, and primarily speak Korean. However, it is very surprising that half of the second generation participants, who were born in American into an English language environment, reported frequently accessing both Korean and English websites when surfing the internet. One would expect English to play an even more dominant role in their lives, but, although they generally text in Korean and access Korean websites less than their first-and-a-half generation counterparts.

The Korean language maintains its importance and centrality even among the second generation youths. These results imply a complex and multifaceted relationship that these children of Korean immigrants have with texting and internet consumption, which for them is bilingual and thus bi-cultural and which brings them greater opportunities to explore and negotiate their ethnic identities as residents of the U.S. in more dynamic and creative ways that are not dependent on location (Tan, 2005).

Table 6.2. Surfing the Internet.

| | Generation Status | | |
|---|---|---|---|
| Websites Often Visited | 1.5 (%) | 2nd (%) | Total (%) |
| Korean websites | 6 (21.4) | 11 (8.7) | 17 (11) |
| English websites | 0 (0) | 57 (45.2) | 57 (37) |
| Both websites | 22 (78.6) | 58 (46.1) | 80 (52) |
| Total | 28 (100) | 126 (100) | 154 (100) |

Moreover, the survey contained a question designed to determine if participants think watching Korean TV programs improves their Korean language fluency. Over half of all participants either agreed or strongly agreed that watching Korean TV programs improves their Korean language fluency, suggesting a strong belief for many that Korean media consumption is vital to their maintaining a link with their Korean culture and reflecting a desire for bilingualism that may further influence their ethnic identities (see Table 6.3).

Of interest here is that only a few first-and-a-half generation participants strongly agreed that watching Korean TV programs improves their Korean language fluency compared to a quarter of second generation participants who shared the same opinion. Also, half of the first-and-a-half generation participants, twice the percentage of the second generation, chose "Neutral" on this question. One explanation for these stark differences might be that first-and-a-half generation participants felt proficient enough in the language since they learned it to a degree as children in Korea before migrating to the U.S. with their family. To expand upon that disparity further, actively consuming Korean TV programs could be a means by which the first-and-a-half generation participants avoid losing, as opposed to improve upon, the high degree of proficiency they have already attained.

Table 6.3. Improving Korean Language by Watching Korean TV Programs.

| | Generation Status | | |
|---|---|---|---|
| Level of Agreement | 1.5 (%) | 2nd (%) | Total (%) |
| Strongly Disagree | 1 (3.6) | 7 (5.6) | 8 (5.2) |
| Disagree | 3 (10.7) | 11 (8.7) | 14 (9.1) |
| Neutral | 14 (50) | 31 (24.6) | 45 (29.2) |
| Agree | 6 (21.4) | 47 (37.3) | 53 (34.4) |
| Strongly Agree | 4 (14.3) | 30 (23.8) | 34 (22.1) |
| Total | 28 (100) | 126 (100) | 154 (100) |

In terms of their own media consumption and language inclinations, while a few interviewees see Korean news and K-pop culture as irrelevant to their lives in the U.S., most are immersing themselves in it as a means to enhance their Korean language fluency and strengthen ethnic pride. Here, the survey results from Tables 6.1, 6.2, and 6.3 corroborate findings from PEIs of interviewees making ample use of digital technologies to maintain Korean language proficiency by staying up to date with K-pop culture. Despite the disproportionately large pool of second generation participants in the survey sample, it is surprising that 60% (77 out of 126) agreed or strongly agreed that watching Korean TV programs improves Korean language proficiency, as it indicates an attachment to Korean media stronger than previously thought for second-generation immigrants.

The literature on ethnic media consumption finds that most adult immigrants, especially the first generation, prefer media from their homeland to that from the host country. According to Elias and Lemish (2008), nearly 80% of adult immigrants in Israel watched Russian-language media on a regular basis, meaning that only a quarter regularly engaged with Hebrew-language programming. In the current media environment, made readily accessible with the proliferation of smartphones, this study similarly finds that children of Korean immigrants, both first-and-a-half and second generation, consume Korean-language channels while in the U.S. More importantly, and specifically, it is their conscious exploration of and commitment to K-pop that serves as the backbone of their maintaining bilingualism. Since Korean ethnic identity markers are predicated on language proficiency (Oh, 2012, p. 267), the ability to speak both Korean and English not only underscores the compatibility of ethnic identity with assimilation, but it also speaks to the long-term prospects of maintaining bi-cultural ethnic identities, which likely stem from engagement with ethnic media.

## References

Alba, R., & Nee, V. (1997). Rethinking assimilation theory for a new era of immigration. *International Migration Review, 31*(4), 826–874.

Elias, N., & Lemish, D. (2008). The Internet life of Former Soviet Union adolescents in Israel. In I. Rydin & U. Sjöberg (Eds.), *Mediated crossroads: Identity, youth culture and ethnicity–Theoretical and methodological challenges* (pp. 173–192). Göteborg, Sweden: Nordicom, Göteborg University.

Gordon, M. (1964). *Assimilation in American life: The role of race, religious, and national origins*. New York, NY: Oxford University Press.

Lee, C. (2004). Korean immigrants' viewing patterns of Korean satellite television and its role in their lives. *Asian Journal of Communication, 14*(1), 68–80.

Lee, J. S. (2006). Exploring the relationship between electronic literacy and heritage language maintenance. *Language Learning and Technology, 10*(2), 93–113

Lemish, D. (2015). *Children and media: A global perspective*. Malden, MA: Wiley-Blackwell Publishing.

Oh, D. (2012). Mediating the boundaries: Second-generation Korean American adolescents' use of transnational Korean media as markers of social boundaries. *International Communication Gazette, 74*(3), 258–276.

Park, K. (2009). *Korean immigrant women and the renegotiation of identity: Class, gender, and the politics of identity*. El Paso, TX: LFB Scholarly Publishing.

Park, R. E. (1928). Human migration and the marginal man. *American Journal of Sociology, 33*(6), 881–893.

Song, A. M. (2003). *Choosing ethnic identity*. Cambridge, UK: Polity Press.

Tan, S.-H. (Ed.). (2005). *Challenging citizenship: Group membership and cultural identity in a global age*. Burlington, VT: Ashgate.

Warner, W. L., & Srole, L. (1945). *The social systems of American ethnic groups*. New Haven, CT: Yale University Press.

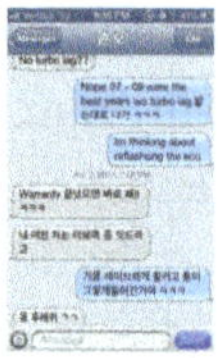

Figure 6.1. A Mixture of English and Korean Languages With My Korean American Friend.
Source: Photo by David.

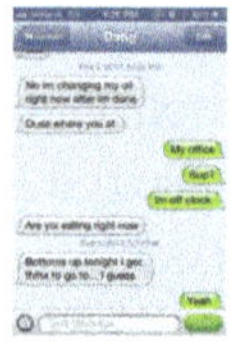

Figure 6.2. Texting Only in English With My American Friend.
Source: Photo by David.

Figure 6.3. Both American and Korean Songs on My iPod.
Source: Photo by Min Joon.

Figure 6.4. Psy.
Source: Photo by Sun.

Figure 6.5. My Korean-English Bible.
Source: Photo by Jun Soo.

Figure 6.6. A Hardworking Korean American.
Source: Photo by Jun Soo.

Figure 6.7. My Precious Bible.
Source: Photo by Lana.

# CONCLUSION

## The Contribution of Digital Media to Segmented Assimilation Theory

This study addressed three specific research questions posed at the outset. First, what is the nature of the digital media practices of first-and-a-half and second generation descendants of Korean immigrants in their socialization and the development of their ethnic identity (see Chapter Three)? Second, how do they engage in the exploration of and commitment to their ethnic identity using the digital media devices at their disposal (see Chapter Four)? Third, based on that relationship between ethnic identity formation and exploration and commitment via digital media, how does digital media consumption affect this young population's assimilation into mainstream American society (see Chapters Five and Six)? A multi-methodological approach, using a combination of PEIs and surveys, provided us additional analytical leverage in addressing digital media practices and their role played in the multifaceted dimensions of ethnic identity formation among the children of Korean immigrants in the U.S.

This final chapter then continues with a discussion of the study's implications, specifically how its examination of digital media practices by the children of Korean immigrants reveals what previous literature has overlooked regarding their ethnic identity formation and how it is poised to fill in that gap.

## The Nature of the Digital Media Practices

In response to the first research question, first-and-a-half and second generation participants showed little difference in their digital media practices. On the one hand, in many ways, they are no different from all other immigrant and non-immigrant children. Just like American teens as discussed in previous research (Madden, Lenhart, Duggan, Cortesi, & Gasser, 2013; Rideout, 2016), they all reported that a variety of digital media technologies, especially smartphones, have become an integral part of their daily routine. Indeed, in terms of technology access, the results of the survey data in this study indicated that smartphones outpaced all other digital technologies as the most frequently accessed internet platform among the children of Korean immigrants. Of the 154 participants, the vast majority reported that they often use smartphones compared to desktop or laptop computer. This result represents another similarity with American teens in that first-and-a-half and second generation interviewees frequently interact with diverse technologies simultaneously in order to form or maintain their social interactions (Rideout, 2016). Furthermore, the way they use these devices is also very diverse, including simultaneous streaming, uploading, recording, listening, sharing, and communicating.

On the other hand, the results of this study also revealed that participants' digital media practices differ from American teens' in numerous respects. The children of Korean immigrants are at a crossroads between two cultures, and the refusal of many to choose one at the expense of the other is reflected in interviewees' digital media practices as they engage with their culture of origin. There are two important phenomena that should be noted. First, smartphone use was nearly ubiquitous among the survey participants, and even though Facebook was reported as the most frequent text messaging application among most of the participants regardless of generation status, both first-and-a-half and second generation participants also strongly favored KakaoTalk as an important text messaging application. When breaking responses down by generation, more than four-fifths of the first-and-a-half generation participants and three quarters of the second generation participants reported using KakaoTalk as their text messaging application. Although it ranked behind Facebook as the second most frequently used texting application for both groups of participants, its lower adoption rate among mainstream American teens suggests that its popularity in this study has important cultural significance that can help fill in gaps in the existing body of research.

The second distinction is that these participants rely extensively on KakaoTalk to keep in touch with local co-ethnic friends as well as family and friends in Korea. Again breaking responses down by generation, the vast majority of the first-and-a-half generation participants reported using it many times a day while almost half of the second generation participants reported the same frequency of use. As already suggested in the survey analysis, one explanation for this difference might be that the former spent at least some of their formative years in Korea, during which they made close personal friends with whom they want or feel the need to keep in touch with after relocating to the U.S. For example, during the PEIs, Rose (17, F, Rural) described how KakaoTalk best enabled her to keep in touch with her friends in Korea, which in turn allowed her relationships with them to continue to grow even after her immigration. Similarly, David's (17, M, Rural) KakaoTalk-centered life effectively transforms his social interactions to make it seem as if he still resides in Korea. These two examples from the first-and-a-half generation reveal the complexities of immigrant children's digital social interactions, and they differ from mainstream American teens as well as their second generation counterparts. After all, neither has left their permanent locus in the American social environment or migrated to one with an unfamiliar culture, whereas the first-and-a-half generation is concerned with maintaining social and cultural links they have left behind.

Of course, for many first-and-a-half generation interviewees as well as some in the second generation, KakaoTalk is a way to connect with their parents' culture. For the former, it preserves the nostalgic feeling of living in Korea with their family and friends. For the latter, it expands or even adds additional social and cultural links to their newfound social and cultural interests, a point that previous research has neglected to explore regarding the second generation. For example, Jackie (15, F, City) described how she set up a KakaoTalk account for her mother so that she could stay connected with her family in Korea through exchanging photographs and sending regular updates about family news and activities. In turn, her mother's engagement with KakaoTalk then encouraged Jackie to expand her own KakaoTalk use and keep her mother's family, whom she has never met face-to-face, an essential part of her daily life. This form of collaboration between immigrant children and parents working as teams around digital technologies was highlighted in previous ethnographic research on Mexican immigrant families (Katz, 2014). Relying on Vygotsky's situated learning theory and the concept of scaffolding (Vygotsky, 1978), Katz argues that scaffolding is a two-way process in immigrant families, with children and parents supporting each other's integration needs. Our study supports Katz's argument that children do not act as independent brokers of technology for their immigrant families, as has been argued in the past, but engage collaboratively, with everyone bringing to family life their unique knowledge and experience.

The two increasingly common phenomena described above defy the core belief of classical assimilation theory, which neglects the value and sustainability of ethnic minority cultures and thus overlooks the positive role that ethnic groups and their cultural assets play in immigrants' adaptation processes (Salomone, 2010). They also provide support to Lievrouw and Livingstone's (2006) argument that far beyond the recognizable proliferation of new technologies that are frequently associated with media, and even beyond the social media networks and geo-locational mobile applications and their informational and communication functions, digital media need to be considered in their contexts of use and the larger societal arrangements. Under the influence of digital media technologies, these children of Korean immigrants not only communicate more regularly with their families and friends overseas, but they also maintain and further develop their ethnic identities thanks to the diverse experiences afforded to them by KakaoTalk. In concert with the existing body of literature, then, this study helps paint a more complete picture of immigrant youths by providing qualitative and quantitative evidence of their intercultural, digital communicative practices to sustain connections with cultures of origin. For example, Yi (2009) discussed how back-and-forth communication with both Korean and American contacts by a local community of Korean American teenagers in the Midwestern U.S. shows a "plentiful blending" of Korean and English, while Salomone (2010) revealed the same cultural flexibility with regard to other immigrant groups despite their feet being firmly planted in the U.S. However, this study more clearly demonstrates the depth of digital communication by the children of Korean immigrants in the U.S. It goes beyond a cultural back-and-forth and instead involves daily, meaningful contact with local co-ethnic friends and friends and family overseas, constituting the processes of ethnic identity exploration and commitment that will be discussed in further detail below.

## Exploring and Committing to Ethnic Identity via Digital Media Devices

In response to the second research question, the results of this study indicate that the first-and-a-half and second generations are not so distinct from one another. Instead, all of the interviewees and survey participants are similar in that ethnic identity is foremost in their minds and that digital media technology has been an integral part of their daily lives. The results further showed the relationship between those two factors, specifically how both generations were already using digital media to negotiate their place in the world with respect to their culture of origin. Looking at their responses during the PEIs more closely, however, shows the different ways they perceive and derive meaning from their experiences with digital media. Some reported using digital media to either explore or commit to their ethnic identity while others reported using it for both exploration and commitment. No matter their activity, though, they frequently reported in their own words the ways in which they are connected to or disconnected from their ethnic identity.

While many participants in past studies have expressed difficulty with exploration, in part because they lacked the necessary resources (Wakefield & Hudley, 2007), the children of Korean immigrants in this study were found to be a notable exception. In past decades, with no internet, smartphones, or SNSs with which to stay culturally informed or communicate at the touch of a button with family and friends in their homeland, immigration was a more permanent and complete commitment (Salomone, 2010). Today, however, this study shows it to be a far different and much more flexible experience. Aided by smartphones, these teens can explore different aspects of their original culture or their ethnic identity online, single out and latch onto anything of interest, and then join social media spaces that allow them to fulfill those interests (Gardner & Davis, 2013). Indeed, interviewees repeatedly expressed their intention to use the power of digital media technology to explore their ethnic identity from multiple perspectives.

As discussed previously, while those in the first-and-a-half generation were born in Korea and have migrated to the U.S., meaning they have spent enough of their formative years in both Korea and the U.S. to know both cultures, those in the second generation were born to immigrant Korean parents in the U.S., suggesting that their exposure to American culture from birth is initially the strongest influence on their identity construction. Regardless of their status, however, most interviewees in this study reported facing challenges that arise from what they perceive as having to choose between their own unique identity and social acceptance. More specifically, in the event of a cultural or social conflict, whether something as benign as a language barrier or as serious as stereotyping/discrimination, they might grow concerned about their ethnic identities because such identities stand out when in conflict with mainstream American culture. Since identity confusion was a common experience for nearly all interviewees at least "at some point" in their lives, they reported that when they became interested in their original culture or ethnic identity, they attempted to explore it using their digital media devices.

During the PEIs, several interviewees reported that they experienced "a critical moment," what developmental psychologists define as the moment that compels individuals to take the initiative in learning about their ethnic identities (Joshi, 2006). These interviewees tended to describe such moments as those times when they discovered their own interest in an aspect of their culture of origin or ethnic identity that they had formerly overlooked. For them, exploration was the product of an intense desire to chart their own course in navigating their ethnic identity. For example, as discussed earlier in the PEI analyses, Eddie's case (16, M, Metro) adequately summarizes many second generation interviewees' two contrasting cultural worlds, which for them necessitates further ethnic identity exploration and negotiation to reconcile the two. According to Eddie, who revealed the critical moment that motivated his own ethnic identity exploration, listening to a catchy pop song from Girls' Generation over KakaoTalk was not just K-pop consumption, but the beginning of his engagement with his cultural heritage. Eddie's case perfectly illustrates the sophistication with which exploring, consuming, and discussing Korean cultural content via digital media enhance his engagement with his parents' culture and give him the platform to learn and explore what it means to be someone who possesses the cultural values and perspectives both of his parents and of America.

Similar to Eddie's case, when discussing her emerging interest in her ethnic background, Ivy (17, F. Metro) described how not being able to answer her friends' questions about North-South Korean tensions due to her lack of knowledge made her feel guilty. When they came with still more questions, she was motivated to move beyond her surface-level familiarity with Korean culture and began looking deeper into Korean history, culture, and traditions. For Ivy, this was her critical moment, the turning point at which she became invested in learning about her ethnic identity. Fully aware of and fluent in the internet's diverse array of resources, she relied heavily on Google and YouTube in her investigation into North and South Korean culture, and, throughout her investigation, she simultaneously became aware of aspects of her own ethnic identity that she had previously overlooked and found new ways to connect with her ethnic heritage. She even credited her online search with convincing her that her ethnic identity should play a larger role in her life. Thus, both Eddie's and Ivy's cases—representative of many second generation interviewees—support the claims by social constructionists that native-born adolescents are likelier to maintain or adopt American identities over time, but that numerous factors may also steer them away from American-made labels, meaning that ethnic self-identity is also likely to change over time (Barth, 1969; Hein, 1994; Lal, 2001; Omi & Winant, 1994; Tuan, 1998).

According to Phinney and Ong (2007) and Wakefield and Hudley (2007), getting to know and interacting with local co-ethnic friends or friends and family overseas is another characteristic of the exploration stage for immigrant youth. For example, during the PEIs, Jieun (17, F, City) reported that she was able to locate and reach out through Facebook to another local American-born co-ethnic friend named Karis. Karis then gave Jieun, who regretted spending much of her early childhood rejecting anything to do with Korea, emotional support in negotiating her own ethnic identity, including teaching and sharing with her what she knew about Korean culture. When describing their online conversations, Jieun reported that they not only discussed news and current events in America, but also the various happenings in Korea as well as Korean popular culture, including K-pop, drama/movies, and even celebrity gossip. Based on her discussion, forming and maintaining her relationship with Karis via Facebook exposed her to more about her own ethnic heritage. Therefore, socialization and the consumption of Korean popular culture, which simultaneously occur in this case in the particular context of Facebook, combine to function as a source of motivation for her to both explore her ethnic culture and discover her own ethnic identity.

Annie (14, F, Rural) may have been born in Korea, but her case nevertheless parallels Jieun's in demonstrating the importance of socialization. She described how meeting her first local co-ethnic friend, Sophia, on Facebook was a positive experience that lessened the culture shock she was feeling after her first day at school in America. Based on her discussion, however, their Facebook-enabled friendship and socialization was mutually beneficial. On one hand, it assisted Annie's integration into her host culture. On the other hand, Annie in turn became Sophia's window to life in Korea, a country she has never actually visited. It seems that by using their familiarity with either Korean or American culture as a form of cultural capital, sharing it with one another then validates their relationship as one of mutual cultural interest that influences their ethnic identities. While both Annie and Sophia relied on each other as cultural resources about Korea and America, respectively, it was Facebook that both linked them and facilitated their socialization.

Annie's case refers broadly to the children of Korean immigrants living in the U.S., but the results overall mirror research into other immigrant communities as well. Russian immigrant children in Israel, for example, have demonstrated the same dynamic use of digital media to integrate into their host culture while simultaneously maintaining their original culture (Elias & Lemish, 2009). This process of inward (host culture) and outward (home culture) integration in which immigrant families are engaged (Elias & Lemish, 2008b) is greatly aided in the present by the use of media more generally, including subscriptions to cable and satellite television channels, internet providers, and mobile media services. Annie's case is therefore part of a broader phenomenon, and it demonstrates the creativity and flexibility with which these interviewees leverage Facebook as a means to locate, connect with, and socialize with co-ethnic peers. This not only eases their own integration into American culture, but it creates a bi-directional, mutually beneficial relationship of cultural exchange in that each person fulfills the other's cultural interests.

At the start of the second decade of the new millennium, terms such as "Facebook revolution" and "Twitter revolution" have become more common, conceptualizing the notions of "dynamic media" as potentially innovative, pervasive, and socially transformative (Cheong, Martin, & Macfadyen, 2012, p. 1). As of June, 2018, reliable statistical reports showed that there are approximately four billion internet users around the world (Internet World Stats, 2018). Contrary to previous decades in which internet users were predominantly located in parts of Europe and North America, the largest number of internet users is now located in Asia, with rapidly growing rates also noticed in Latin America, the Middle East, and Africa (Cheong et al., 2012, p. 3). Today, YouTube is one of the most influential platforms of the digital media landscape. Launched in February of 2005, YouTube became an online repository where each individual can upload, share, watch, and discuss video clips. The platform has radically transformed how society consumes, produces, circulates, and integrates media content into our daily lives (Ng, 2012, p. 266).

Based on the rich data gathered from the interviewees, although their degree of digital media engagement may differ from one another, digital media technology has become their most important tool for exploring diverse aspects of their cultural heritage and adopting those aspects into their ethnic identity. So, while their co-ethnic friends sometimes play a great role in introducing them to Korean popular culture, digital media technology gives them the space to navigate it and then expand and share their interest with others (Kim & Kim, 2011). Consuming these media is therefore more than just a hobby; it is a cultural learning experience, an educational pursuit in which the children of Korean immigrants can connect with their ethnic identity as they dive further into Korean popular culture (Huat & Iwabuchi, 2008).

Thus, we found that a strong aspect of ethnic identity commitment as described by interviewees was constant Korean popular culture consumption (K-pop, TV dramas, entertainment shows, movies, etc.) using their digital media devices. More specifically, during the PEIs, some interviewees described the process of seeking out Korean popular culture online (YouTube, for example) using their digital media device as exploring this aspect of their ethnic identity. However, when it came to commitment, others reported going beyond consumption to depending heavily on Korean popular media as a way to stay informed about Korean culture. Such investment in Korean culture and media consumption for the purposes of ethnic identity commitment was a distinctive characteristic among both first-and-a-half and second generation participants. These findings are similar to Subramanian's (2010) study of young South Asian American women, which described their preference for media including night time soap operas and Bollywood films as a way to uphold their ethnic identity. Furthermore, just like those young South Asian American women, interviewees in this study are Americanized to a certain extent, but they nevertheless consume Korean popular culture as a way to remain tied to their ethnic identity despite adopting particular values and norms of American society into their identities.

Survey participants' easy access to Korean popular culture through digital media draws attention to the content that they then choose to consume, particularly how that content helps them negotiate with a variety of aspects of their ethnic identity. This key finding also illustrates how the free circulation of popular culture across national boundaries is increasingly facilitating new links among people around the world, especially youths (Ju, 2007). Popular culture consumption, such as watching Korean TV dramas and listening to K-pop, is a significant part of youths' leisure activities (Kim, 2009). In other words, the global consumption of popular culture has become another distinct social element of the young generation, and digital media have become an efficient and simple way to promote this consumption (Kim & Kim, 2011).

With regard to first-and-a-half generation participants, the three most commonly explored topics were "Korean drama, variety/reality shows, movies, or clips" (almost all respondents), "News and current events in Korea" (over three-quarters), and "K-pop" (three-quarters). Second generation participants differed in their top three preferences: "Korean drama, variety/reality shows, movies, or clips" (over three-quarters), "Korean celebrities" (about two-fifths), and "K-pop" (over half). According to these results, both groups of participants immerse themselves in a wide variety of Korean entertainment media, which is consistent with the results of the PEIs. Past studies have shown distinctions between first-and-a-half and second generation groups in terms of their orientation towards their culture of origin, but, according to this study, Korean popular media appear to transcend those distinctions. Indeed, when Korean popular media are considered, there was little variation between the groups, since the majority of both groups named it as their most frequent interest, suggesting that digital media technology plays the same or a similar role with regard to their exploration of their original culture or ethnic identity. Furthermore, consistent with Lin, Song, and Ball-Rokeach's (2010) research, digital media technology and K-pop content enable them to rise above their current social and cultural limitations and to seek out new content experiences, no matter whether that content is Korean news stories, K-pop, movies, TV dramas, or a mix of media (Lin et al., 2010). Thus, the content most commonly explored online by the survey participants reflects, at least in part, their desires to explore and form emotional ties with their culture of origin or ethnic identity.

Throughout the analysis presented in the book, we discussed the youths participating in the study in a unified manner and did not refer to any gender differences. The reason for this choice is that an interesting finding of the study was the absence of any significant gender differences in responses to all questions in the questionnaire related to ethnic identity as well as to most related to media use. The only statistically significant differences found were much more in line with the established literature on gender differences in media use more generally (see for example Lemish, 2015): female teens in this study used smartphones more than male teens, while male teens played video game consoles and used Skype more than female teens. Also not surprisingly, female teens watched Korean TV dramas and variety and reality shows more than their male counterparts. We thus concluded that the ethnic-identity issues over shadowed potential gender differences in relationship to the topic of this study.

## First-and-a-Half and Second Generation Commitment to Ethnic Identity

One of the most striking findings of this study is that there is only a limited difference between the first-and-a-half and second generation in their commitment to their ethnic identity. Just as they both turn to their digital media technology to explore compelling aspects of their ethnic identity as in the examples above, they both also tended to express ethnic identity commitment online. SNSs in particular are their primary means of foregrounding their ethnic identities and cultural tastes, which include posting comments, status updates, and sharing photos with friends in what they see as a casual and relaxed digital environment. In so doing, they are expressing salient aspects of their ethnic identity on their SNS profiles for others to see and interpret. In the eyes of the interviewees, this public foregrounding of their investment in their ethnic identity online is seen as a form of commitment.

For example, during the PEIs, Ha Sun (17, F, Metro), who favors a Korean identity over an American one, described her commitment to her ethnic identity by showing a photo of her Korean map, one of her Facebook photos. She may live in America, but her picture of this map indicates that America is not the foundation of her identity. She identifies as Korean and claims Korea, instead of her current country of residence, as her home. In this context, then, the photo is the visual representation of her ethnic identity. Thus, Ha Sun's case shows the way SNSs play a major role in giving her an outlet to express what she values in terms of her ethnic identity, such as a photo of her Korean map.

Suji (15, F, Metro) similarly discussed how two of her Facebook pictures represent her ethnic identity in all its complexity as well as the two different cultural and social worlds that she values. The first is of a white chocolate mocha from Starbucks, which speaks to her American cultural values, and the second is of *potbingsoo*, which instead speaks to her Korean cultural values. Both photos represent different facets of her identity, revealing in her case how she uses Facebook as a public space to bridge the cultures of which she is a part and show what she values about her unique ethnic identity.

In John's case (15, M, Metro), he showed three photos that demonstrate his comfort in two different groups: An American high school soccer team and his group of Korean friends. His routine online behavior, including posting pictures of the soccer player Ji Sung Park and the Korean national flag on his Facebook page, reflects his ethnic pride and his intention to show that pride as he makes visible his ethnic identity. However, it is noteworthy that his Facebook page contains photos of both American and Korean cultural elements, thus playing a vital role in helping him build "a newly emerging hybrid cultural realm" (Elias & Lemish, 2008a, p. 173) that mixes his American and Korean influences into a unique expression of his ethnic identity.

While Ha Sun, Suji, and John are representative of those interviewees who felt that Facebook empowers them to express commitment to their ethnic identity, their cases also show how such expressions are made in concert with the social bonding that takes place through the sharing of photos. Indeed, as these teens capture and share their daily life experiences with increasing creativity thanks to smartphones, it is clear that the smartphone has become a kind of amplifier, a means for these youths to claim and visually express their identities as they socialize with others on SNSs (Ling, 2007).

Moreover, the act of sharing photos on Facebook is a public invitation for others to comment on and evaluate them as well, regardless of their relationship to or understanding of a particular photo's context. As such, the interviewees' pictures themselves are meaningful, but so were the comments they received from their friends. For instance, in the case of Suji, the photo of *potbingsoo* was greeted positively by her co-ethnic friends because they also had a personal, cultural connection to this Korean traditional dessert stemming from their own childhoods. Sharing the photo of *potbingsoo* online thus gave her the opportunity to strengthen her relationship with co-ethnic friends through a sort of collective nostalgia. Also, in John's case, his friends showed their overwhelming support for his decision to virtually fly the Korean flag in foregrounding his ethnic identity on his Facebook page. As he explained, his Korean American and even non-Korean friends' positive comments have only motivated him further to use Facebook as a means to showcase his ethnic identity. When examined in the context of Livingstone (2008), SNSs become outlets of expression in which Suji and John are visible to their friends and where they can experiment with projections of themselves based on their peers' reactions. As described in both cases above, the positive reinforcement that they receive from their friends acts as an incentive for ever stronger commitment to their ethnic identity.

During the PEIs, it became apparent that a portion of interviewees have transformed their SNSs into personalized and hybridized spaces composed of both Korean and American cultural elements and where they can share their experiences with both cultures. Unlike American mainstream teenagers, in some respects, their SNS use doubles as a means to engage with their ethnic heritage, to share their views of what it means for them to be Korean. Their use of SNSs is therefore anything but routine as it simultaneously gives them a way to foreground their personal tastes and ethnic identities (boyd, 2007) and reflect on those identities even while they are exploring and committing to them (Rosen, 2010). SNS use for these teens is not just a matter of back-and-forth communication, but it is a significant and meaningful way for them to continuously negotiate the complexity of their ethnic identities and to express those identities in increasingly creative ways (Wardyga, 2012).

Phinney and Ong (2007) and Wakefield and Hudley (2007) state that a strong attachment to one's own ethnic culture is characteristic of the commitment stage. According to this study, out of 154 survey participants, a third watch Korean drama/movies and about half watch Korean TV variety shows at least occasionally or very frequently, numbers that suggest a strong attachment to Korean culture that then influences participants' perceptions of their ethnic identities. In terms of that consumption, interviewees stated during the PEIs that accessing YouTube via their smartphones was their primary source for Korean popular media. This is overwhelmingly supported by the survey data, which revealed that the vast majority of participants reported using YouTube as their social media site. For example, Min Joon (15, M, Metro) and Sun (15, M, Rural) described frequently accessing K-pop and Korean drama/movies via YouTube. For these and other interviewees, watching Korean dramas or movies constituted a family activity, a way to both maintain traditional rituals and celebrations while in their host country and share in a collective nostalgia for the same activity when they resided in their home country (Salomone, 2010). This example of what has been coined "Sunday Culture" (Lemish, Drotner, Liebes, Maigret, & Stald, 1998) is another illustration of the many ways families come together to engage with media in the process of integration and identity formation. However, regardless of the content and how it was accessed and consumed, all interviewees considered this digital media practice as a way to better understand Korean culture as being integral to their ethnic identity.

As David, one of the interviewees cited above, explained his digital media practice, "Using my smartphone, I watch Korean media like I eat Korean food here." Indeed, for the majority of interviewees, consuming Korean popular culture is as ordinary a part of their daily routine as eating meals, suggesting that emotional and mental nourishment is just as fundamental to their being as physical nourishment. Beyond consumption, though, many interviewees talked about the knowledge gained from consuming Korean popular culture and how that influenced both how they see themselves and how they are perceived by those inside and outside their ethnic community. Those interviewees who claimed a strong commitment to their ethnic identity in terms of the amount of Korean media they consume would commonly follow that up by stating their favorite Korean song, drama, movie, or even their favorite Korean celebrity.

In stark contrast to that intense level of commitment, a few interviewees did report a lack of interest in their ethnic identity. On one hand, some interviewees equated that choice with the general decision to distance themselves from their ethnic identity. On the other hand, other interviewees discussed their intention to consume more Korean popular culture if only because it is what they perceive that their co-ethnic and non-Korean peers expect. Overall, however, the findings suggest that interviewees view regular consumption of Korean popular culture as an essential way to forge their ethnic identity. They therefore placed great importance on digital media technology as it revolutionized how they consume Korean media and stay connected to Korea, keeping open cultural links to Korea that continually influence their ethnic identity formation.

One important takeaway from both the interviews and survey responses is not just that digital media technology is a daily part of these teens' lives, but that it emerged as the most critical element in helping them stay engaged in exploring their ethnic identity, committing to it, or both. In terms of that exploration and commitment, using the MEIM–R instrument's cumulative scale, the first-and-a-half generation had quite similar means. Both groups therefore appear strongly engaged in exploration and commitment with regards to navigating their ethnic identity despite a minor decline in numbers among the second generation. Furthermore, even though they now live in their local communities in the U.S., their engagement with digital media technology in service of their ethnic identity may alter their daily lives as they begin and continue to incorporate Korean cultural elements into their ethnic identities.

These findings are much in line with research arguing that immigrant families in the U.S. demonstrate a different pattern of media consumption (e.g., television) compared to the white population (Lemish, 2007). As the range of media available to immigrant families in the U.S. becomes richer and wider, these families display distinct patterns of media use because of their special needs. An example of this unique media consumption manner can be seen in the way in which immigrants and their children, the latter of whom are well-versed in global media technologies, use ethnic media as means to retain connections with their countries of origin (Appadurai, 1996). In some cases, it was not so much about sustaining the connection with their cultural homeland itself that was valuable, but the continuation of activities that the family used to enjoy before their migration. In some families, particularly for descendants of immigrants, ethnic media can also offer a way of learning about their parents' native language (de Block & Buckingham, 2007). In this sense, using ethnic media, immigrants and their children can access their own culture whenever and wherever they need because the proliferation of satellite and cable television and online networks ensure that media content is globally shared (Brinkerhoff, 2009). Some scholars argue that more exposure to ethnic media in the U.S. prevents immigrants from obtaining necessary information about a new host country and acquiring the host language proficiency, resulting in less integration into the host country. However, several research findings assert that immigrants prefer to use their ethnic language media because these ethnic media provide more relevant information and resources about becoming accustomed to their surroundings in a new culture (Elias & Lemish, 2008a; Lee & Tse, 1994). In other words, ethnic media can provide the immigrants and their children, both of whom suffer from a lack of host language proficiency, the opportunity to learn new cultural ways through one's native language rather than through the host language until one has enough host language skills (Mansfield-Richardson, 2000; Subervi-Velez, 1986).

## Korean American Youth and Segmented Assimilation

In light of the above data, we dispute the popular assimilationist viewpoint that immigrants and their descendants become ever more assimilated the longer they reside in the U.S., which suggests they unilaterally adopt American culture without question or deviation. Both groups reported that they use digital media technology to engage in exploration of and commitment to their ethnic identity in increasingly creative ways that thanks to their devices' diverse functions. Ethnic identity exploration for both groups, for example, tended to mean using digital media technology to locate, stream/download, and learn more about Korean popular culture. However, parallel to this exploration by intense consumption, they simultaneously make use of the social aspects of digital media technology to create and share content (from photos to virtual spaces such as Facebook profiles) and contribute to discussions about content by commenting and voicing their opinions, which for them equates to commitment to their ethnic identity. Just like other contemporary Asian American groups in the U.S. as discussed in Song's (2003) research, the results of this study make quite clear that the children of Korean immigrants in the U.S., by virtue of their exploration of and commitment to their ethnic identity, represent a rejection of the linear model of assimilation and the belief that such immigrants will inevitably abandon their original culture's norms, beliefs, and traditions in favor of American values and an American identity (Brinkerhoff, 2009).

In response to the last research question, it became clear in interviews that both first-and-a-half and second generation immigrants have mastered both English and Korean even as they have preserved a cultural anchor in their parents' ethnic heritage. Similar to the findings in Park's (2009) study, both groups described during the PEIs how they frequently alternate back-and-forth between English and Korean to communicate with different groups of friends. In the case of the first-and-a-half generation group, they made it quite clear that their regular, everyday use of English does not equate to diminished Korean language abilities. Even though their living environment has physically and socially changed as a result of relocating to the U.S., they indeed seem reluctant to lose their Korean language proficiency. For example, as shown via a smartphone screenshot during the PEIs, David (17, M, Rural) communicates extensively with his parents, who are currently living in Korea, via KakaoTalk, and he does so exclusively in Korean. In his second screenshot, his Korean American friend's screen name is written in Korean, and there is a plentiful mix of English and Korean in the messages they exchange with each other. In contrast to his first and second smartphone screenshots, David's third photo shows his American friend's screen name—written in English—as well as an English-only conversation. During his interview, he was able to express his complex thoughts and emotions in English as well as in Korean, demonstrating a remarkably good command of the Korean language.

David's diverse efforts to preserve his Korean language proficiency, motivated by a strong reluctance to lose it, parallel the experiences of several other interviewees. For instance, by listening to K-pop via his iPod, Min Joon (15, M, Metro) felt that he is brushing up on his Korean language skills. As shown in a screenshot during the PEIs, there was an eclectic mixture of American and Korean song titles on Min Joon's iPod. Furthermore, Sun (15, M, Rural) was the interviewee who described in detail his intentional consumption of K-pop to prove his Korean language proficiency outside of his ethnic community. This is because he believes that outsiders who know he is a Korean and who are familiar with K-pop would expect him to have that same knowledge and more in addition to Korean language fluency. An important aspect of K-pop consumption for him, then, is that consumption is equivalent to language maintenance, allowing him to show his pride in his Korean language proficiency outside of his ethnic community.

Two second generation interviewees, Jun Soo (16, M, Rural) and Lana (17, F, Metro), showed photos of their own Bibles, both of which were Korean-English, as evidence of their simultaneous mastery of Korean and English even though both of them were born in the U.S. According to them, they learned Korean by attending an after-school Korean private supplementary institution in their neighborhood. However, we also found that their parents strongly influenced their language acquisition by encouraging them to become a part of "Sunday culture" and watch TV programs with them, programs from their former homeland that research shows enhance family togetherness (Lemish, 2015, p. 153). In line with Elias and Lemish's (2008b) study that showed how parents tried to maintain their children's Russian language abilities, what is significant about this portion of their interviews is how proactive their parents were regarding their children's Korean language acquisition. In addition to enrolling them in Korean language schools for in-person, intense language education, they expose them to diverse Korean media on a daily basis as a more casual means of hearing and practicing the language. Since transmission of language is inevitably tied to ethnic identity formation (Phinney, 1990, 1991), fluent bilingualism allows these children to resist—to some degree—assimilation by any one monolithic identity as expected by the classical assimilation model, thereby helping them maintain a more ethnic identity (Sears, Fu, Henry, & Bui, 2003).

As discussed above, most first-and-a-half and second generation interviewees explained the important role that Korean plays in their daily lives. In addition, half of the survey participants reported often visiting both Korean and English websites, suggesting that both have an impact on their ethnic identity. Also, data from the survey indicated that over half of the participants either agreed or strongly agreed that watching Korean TV programs improves their Korean language fluency. This number not only reflects their desire to remain bilingual, but it represents a strong belief for many that in order to maintain a link with their Korean cultural heritage, they must keep up with Korean media. Furthermore, survey data indicates that three-quarters of participants use Korean alongside their regular use of English when they engage in texting, demonstrating again their attempts to remain connected to Korean culture even while living in the U.S. and adapting to American society. As a result, with regards to interviewees' bilingualism, digital media technology has taken on another role in addition to assisting with relationship development and maintenance and ethnic media consumption; it helps these teens to both foster and retain proficiency in their ethnic language.

These findings thus do not support the classical assimilation perspective which argues that the nearly uncontested adoption of English as a common language and the prevalent transition to American ways of life serve as evidence of the contemporary second generation's trajectory of a linear pattern of assimilation. Instead, they support the contrasting evidence presented by Zhou (2001) regarding the particular case of Vietnamese children who did not demonstrate an ideal scenario of a linear, universal adoption of an American identity. Another source of data that reinforces our conclusion that assimilation is not a linear process is the fact that only two participants self-identified as American (1.4%) (see Chapter Four). If the linear model of assimilation, which argues that all immigrants and their descendants will abandon their culture of origin and adopt a pure American identity (Gordon, 1964), was true, more than two participants should have self-identified as "American." Instead, the most commonly reported ethnic group among the participants was Korean American (41.0%), showing consistency with the results of the PEIs, in which 30 of 31 interviewees identified themselves as Korean American. Although they are all positioned between two conflicting cultural forces, they are not necessarily conflicted in that they feel they must choose one or the other. In contrast, they routinely demonstrated the ability to observe American and Korean culture in-depth and subsequently adopt into their core identity those elements from both cultures that speak to their most closely held beliefs, values, and attitudes.

The next most common response was the country-of-origin identity as South Korean or Korean (36.8%). This is consistent with several earlier studies showing that some second generation Asian American children may eventually take their parents' original ethnic identity as their own after initially resisting their ethnic heritage (Min, 2002; Min & Kim, 2000; Thai, 2002).

An examination of the past 100 years of immigration history reveals a stark contrast between two opposing views of what it means to be American: the first, as referenced above, is the rigid idea of linear assimilation while the second is segmented assimilation, which speaks to a more flexible self-identity that mixes one's diverse cultural influences (Salomone, 2010). The results from this study suggest an inconsistency with the pattern of findings observed in prior traditional assimilation literature. Both the PEI and survey analyses about present-day intersections of digital media technology and ethnic identity formation among the children of Korean immigrants provide much stronger evidence to support segmented assimilation. Indeed, this study has demonstrated that the children of Korean immigrants, whether first-and-a-half or second generation, have an easier time than their parents weaving themselves into American society because of their regular social and cultural contact with their homeland even as they keep their feet in their host society, which is referred to as "selective acculturation" (Portes & Rumbaut, 2001). Furthermore, both first-and-a-half and second generation groups were steadfast in their professed Koreanness. Based on this segmented assimilation perspective, the role that digital media devices play in the transmission of culture and language as well as in the formation of ethnic identity has clearly been overlooked by the classical assimilation model.

The existing body of research on segmented assimilation theory has isolated several factors, such as family and ethnic community, that have the potential to influence ethnic identity formation through the transmission of culture and language (Saenz, Hwang, Aguirre, & Anderson, 1995). However, this study has shown that digital media practices add another dimension for consideration as the children of Korean immigrants in the U.S. increasingly use technology to explore and commit to their ethnic identity while looking for ways to bridge their homeland and host society. Indeed, the children of Korean immigrants in the U.S. today are distinct from those in the past in that digital media is an inseparable part of their lives from a very young age, a factor that early assimilationist scholars never could have imagined would be key to ethnic identity development. As previously discussed during the PEIs, most interviewees expressed strong beliefs on the importance of digital media for their own ethnic identity exploration and commitment. As a result, their ethnic identities that used to be location-specific and depend on specific experiences native to those locations are now made flexible by digital media and more apt to transform over time (Fitzgerald, 1992; Xie, 2005).

Finally, we note that despite our expectations to possibly find gender and/or location differences in our sample of young people, these two key identifiers did not surface as significant in our study. When it comes to adults, immigration scholarship to date has demonstrated that not only generational differences, but also gender ones play a role in migration experiences and integration processes (e.g., Hondagneu-Sotelo, 1994; Pessar, 2003). Immigrant women to Israel, for example, have been found to be at a "double disadvantage" for being both women as well as immigrants, as expressed in their lower rate of employment in comparison to immigrant men, weaker language competencies, and weaker networks that can facilitate the double burden of balancing work and family (Semyonov, 1997). However, regarding the immigrant youth in our study and their digital media use and identity formation, we did not find any significant gender differences in any of the variables studied; both boys and girls used their digital devices for the same functions, were highly dependent on them, and expressed very similar attitudes regarding their cultural identity. Similarly, our PEI interviews did not detect any meaningful differences between respondents living in different urban contexts and their digital media use and identity formation. The survey explored only youth from a metropolitan area, so location did not play a role in that source of data.

## Comparing First Generation Korean American Adults With Youth

Our research showed that interviewees and survey participants orient their identity towards both their home country and host society based on their bicultural connections and activities, corroborating Kim's (2018) research on first generation Korean American adults in the Washington-Baltimore metropolitan area, whose use of digital media devices to stay connected to Korean culture influenced their assimilation. As Kim (2018) found, most first generation Korean American interviewees were engaging in regular and occasional conversations about everyday things with friends and family in Korea via KakaoTalk and SNSs on their smartphones. Also, their consumption of Korean ethnic media provided them with common reference points, such as news and current events, about which they could discuss with family members and friends in Korea, helping to sustain ethnic ties and identities. Finally, he noted that first generation Korean Americans are no longer forced to choose between assimilation and preserving their ethnic identity, but instead can pursue both because digital media technologies can serve the dual functions of aiding adaptation and integration and ensuring that such immigrants can stay connected to and immersed in their original culture.

Since Kim's (2018) study has not examined this aspect of digital media practices and their ethnic orientations among first-and-a-half and second generation Korean Americans, our research helps fill in gaps in the existing literature by targeting more diverse groups of younger immigrants as well as larger samples. By statistically analyzing survey responses and performing comparative analyses on the first-and-a-half and second generations' survey responses and PEIs, our research provides myriad implications for our target group's digital media practices and their impact on the direction of assimilation among this group in years to come. In contrast to our prediction that a significant difference would exist between Kim's findings and our own, owing to the age difference between the respective samples, our first-and-a-half and second generation groups showed little difference in their self-reported ethnicity. More importantly, they seem to exhibit a stronger attachment to their home country that is both deeply emotional and personal as well as wholly immersed in the moment-to-moment changes occurring in Korea.

Another similarity with Kim's (2018) findings is the frequent use of KakaoTalk via smartphone in the everyday lives of our participants. Just like those first generation adult Korean Americans, our first-and-a-half and second generation participants also rely extensively on KakaoTalk to keep in touch with local co-ethnic friends as well as family and friends in Korea to stay engaged with their culture of origin. More specifically, their active engagement with Korean culture via KakaoTalk on their smartphones sets their current digital media practices apart from those of the past. These developments suggest that bicultural engagement by the first-and-a-half and second generations will persist in the years to come as their smartphones and applications such as KakaoTalk continue to create stable, almost tangible connections with their home country.

However, one unique distinction from the findings among first generation Korean Americans in Kim's research is the enormous impact of K-pop on the first-and-a-half and second generations in our research and the extent to which a more Americanized or Koreanized way of life emerges with growing bicultural participation. While Kim (2018) found the role of K-pop to be minimal among first generation Korean Americans in his research, we found that K-pop to be deeply pervasive in the everyday lives of the first-and-a-half and second generation. Not only do they frequently consume it and seek out up-to-date information, but also a fair number of interviewees credited with strengthening their Korean pride and identity. The second distinction from first generation Korean Americans in Kim's research is not simply their active effort to establish deeper roots with their culture of origin, but also their strong commitment to expressing their ethnic pride and ethnic identity by posting highly personal content on their KakaoTalk chatrooms and Facebook pages. In fact, although it was also present and pursued by first generation Korean Americans in Kim's (2018) research, these teens' exploration of and commitment to events in their home country, cultural trends, or K-pop via various digital media devices is occurring at a pace and volume that is both quantitatively and qualitatively different precisely because they are significantly more digitally savvy.

In sum, the growing convergence of ethnic identity with using smartphones and KakaoTalk to frequently communicate with family and friends in Korea and consume Korean ethnic media and K-pop is significant for the way it fosters synchronization with daily life in Korea, as found both among Kim's (2018) first generation immigrants and our first-and-a-half and second generation immigrants. Korean immigrants today, unlike past immigrants whose goal was permanent residency in the U.S., are seemingly more oriented to Korea because immigration is seen more as a flexible option as opposed to an irreversible decision (Park, 2009). For them, the instant connectivity with their home country that is enabled by digital media technologies allows for diverse ways to express being American and orient their identity towards the home country and the host society. Therefore, the relationship between the first, first-and-a-half, and second generation Korean immigrants in the U.S. is notable for the ways in which KakaoTalk (specifically its daily role in (re)orienting immigrants to their home country) is blurring the boundaries between those who either lacked cultural competence or whose Koreanness was in any way ever questioned.

## Conclusion

With the ever-changing portrait of the face of Americans, the issue of ethnic identity is increasingly being pushed to the forefront. Producing ethnicity in the U.S. is in constant flux, particularly in the negotiation between how ethnic minorities are identified as ethnic and racial subjects and how they identify themselves as ethnic groups. As presented above, first-and-a-half generation and second generation children of Korean immigrants in the U.S. often stand between two contrasting cultures, necessitating further ethnic identity exploration and negotiation to reconcile them. In the era of digital media technologies, by taking advantage of digital media and communication technologies, these young Korean descendants navigate through the multiple online discourses of race, ethnicity, and culture, and they pick and choose from a diverse array of representations of Koreanness. Immigration is a phenomenon that spans time, generations, and geographies; it has a history. According to Appadurai (1996), historical and political changes have reshaped our notion of immigration. In recent years, scholars have pointed to a number of possible differences between the social contexts of past and contemporary immigration as a basis for arguing that the fate of new immigrant groups will likely differ from that of past groups.

In conclusion, the results of this study challenge the assumptions of early assimilationist scholars, who argued that immigrants undergo a complete and linear adoption of an American identity. Of course, one of the key differences that separates individuals in this study from generations past is that the former were born in the era of digital media and are thus equipped with a variety of digital media technology and the know-how to use it. The prevalence of this technology in the lives of the children of Korean immigrants in the U.S. may therefore help explain their retention of a strong ethnic identity even as they continue to integrate into American society. This simultaneous cultural adaptation and retention is made possible for the children of Korean immigrants in the U.S. by digital media technology precisely because it is their primary means of exploring and committing to their culture of origin and ethnic identity while living in their host society. For them, perceiving the link between digital media technology and ethnic identity was therefore an inevitability; only those who did not grow up with such technology might wonder if the two are connected. Thus, based on the interviewees' and survey participants' responses, we learn that their digital media practices are a critical element in their daily lives. They represent the continued negotiation of their ethnic identities and indeed the very means by which they sustain that ethnic identity in the face of mainstream American culture.

## References

Appadurai, A. (1996). *Modernity at large: Cultural dimensions of globalization*. Minneapolis, MN: University of Minnesota Press.

Barth, F. (1969). *Ethnic groups and boundaries*. Boston, MA: Little, Brown.

boyd, d. m. (2007). Why youth (heart) social network sites: The role of networked publics in teenage social life. In D. Buckingham (Ed.), *Youth, identity, and digital media* (pp. 119–142). Cambridge, MA: MIT Press.

Brinkerhoff, J. M. (2009). *Digital diasporas: Identity and transnational engagement*. Cambridge, UK: Cambridge University Press.

Cheong, P. H., Martin, J. N., & Macfadyen, L. P. (2012). *New media and intercultural communication: Identity, community, and politics*. New York, NY: Peter Lang.

de Block, L., & Buckingham, D. (2007). *Global children, global media: Migration, media and childhood*. New York, NY: Palgrave Macmillan.

Elias, N., & Lemish, D. (2008a). The Internet life of Former Soviet Union adolescents in Israel. In I. Rydin & U. Sjöberg (Eds.), *Mediated crossroads: Identity, youth culture and ethnicity–Theoretical and methodological challenges* (pp. 173–192). Göteborg, Sweden: Nordicom, Göteborg University.

Elias, N., & Lemish, D. (2008b). Media uses in immigrant families: Torn between "inward" and "outward" paths of integration. *International Communication Gazette, 70*(1), 21–40.

Elias, N., & Lemish, D. (2009). Spinning the web of identity: Internet's roles in immigrant adolescents' search of identity. *New Media & Society, 11*(4), 533–551.

Fitzgerald, T. K. (1992). Media, ethnicity, and identity. In P. Scannell, P. Schlesinger, & C. Spark (Eds.), *Culture and power: A media, culture & society reader* (pp. 112–133). London: Sage Publications.

Gardner, H., & Davis, K. (2013). *The app generation: How today's youth navigate identity, intimacy, and imagination in a digital world.* New Haven, CT: Yale University Press.

Gordon, M. (1964). *Assimilation in American life: The role of race, religion, and national origins.* New York, NY: Oxford University Press.

Hein, J. (1994). From migrant to minority: Hmong refugees and the social construction of identity in the United States. *Sociological Inquiry*, 64(3), 281–306.

Hondagneu-Sotelo, P. (1994). *Gendered transitions: Mexican experiences of immigration.* Berkeley, CA: University of California Press.

Huat, C. B., & Iwabuchi, K. (Eds.). (2008). *East Asian pop culture: Analysing the Korean wave.* Hong Kong: Hong Kong University Press.

Hyejung, J. (2007). The nature of nationalism in the "Korean wave": A framing analysis of news coverage about Korean pop culture. In *Conference Papers–National Communication Association* (Vol. 1).

Internet World Stats. (2018). World internet usage and population statistics. Retrieved from http://www.internetworldstats.com/stats.htm

Joshi, K. (2006). *New roots in America's sacred ground.* New Brunswick, NJ: Rutgers University Press.

Katz, V. S. (2014). *Kids in the middle: How children of immigrants negotiate community interactions for their families.* New Brunswick, NJ: Rutgers University Press.

Kim, D. K., & Kim, M.-S. (Eds.). (2011). *Hallyu: Influence of Korean popular culture in Asia and beyond.* Seoul: Seoul National University Press.

Kim, D. Y. (2018). *Transnational communities in the smartphone age: The Korean community in the nation's capital.* Maryland: Lexington Books.

Kim, Y. (2009). *Media consumption and everyday life in Asia.* London: Routledge.

Lal, B. B. (2001). Learning to do ethnic identity. In D. Parker & M. Song (Eds.), *Rethinking "mixed race"* (pp. 154–172). London: Pluto Press.

Lee, W., & Tse, D. (1994). Changing media consumption in a new home: Acculturation patterns among Hong Kong immigrants to Canada. *Journal of Advertising, 23*, 57–71.

Lemish, D. (2007). *Children and television: A global perspective.* Malden, MA: Blackwell Publishing.

Lemish, D. (2015). *Children and media: A global perspective.* Malden, MA: Wiley-Blackwell Publishing.

Lemish, D., Drotner, K., Liebes, T., Maigret, E., & Stald, G. (1998). Global culture in practice: A look at children and adolescents in Denmark, France and Israel. *European Journal of Communication, 13*(4), 539–556.

Lievrouw, L., & Livingstone, S. (Eds.). (2006). *Handbook of new media: Social shaping and social consequences*. Fully revised student edition. London: Sage Publications.

Lin, W.-Y., Song, H., & Ball-Rokeach, S. (2010). Localizing the global: Exploring the transnational ties that bind in new immigrant communities. *Journal of Communication*, *60*(2), 205–229. doi: 10.1111/j.1460-2466.2010.01480.x

Ling, R. (2007). Children, youth, and mobile communication. *Journal of Children and Media*, *1*(1), 60–67.

Livingstone, S. (2008). Internet literacy: Young people's negotiation of new online opportunities. In T. McPherson (Ed.), *Digital youth, innovation, and the unexpected* (pp. 101–122). Cambridge, MA: MIT Press.

Madden, M., Lenhart, A., Duggan, M., Cortesi, S., & Gasser, U. (2013). *Teens and technology 2013*. Washington, D.C.: Pew Research Center.

Mansfield-Richardson, V. (2000). *Asian Americans and the mass media: A content analysis of twenty United States newspapers and a survey of Asian American journalists*. New York, NY: Garland.

Min, P. G. (2002). Introduction. In P. G. Min (Ed.), *The second generation: Ethnic identity among Asian Americans* (pp. 1–18). Walnut Creek, CA: AltaMira Press.

Min, P. G., & Kim, R. (2000). Formation of ethnic and racial identities: Narratives by young Asian-American professionals. *Ethnic and Racial Studies*, *23*(4), 735–760.

Ng, K. (2012). Asian American new media communication as cultural engagement: E-mail, vlog/blogs, mobile applications, social networks, and YouTube. In P. H. Cheong, J. N. Martin, & L. P. Macfadyen (Eds.), *New media and intercultural communication: Identity, community, and politics* (pp. 79–106). New York, NY: Peter Lang.

Omi, M., & Winant, H. (1994). *Racial formation in the United States*. New York, NY: Routledge.

Park, S. (2009). Negotiating identities and re-acculturation of second-generation Korean Americans: The role of ethnic media and peer group dynamics. *Korea Journal*, *49*(1), 61–97.

Pessar, P. (2003). Engendering migration studies: The case of new immigrants in the United States. In P. Hondagneu-Sotelo (Ed.), *Gender and U.S. immigration* (pp. 20–42). Berkeley, CA: University of California Press.

Phinney, J. (1990). Ethnic identity in adolescents and adults: Review of research. *Psychological Bulletin*, *108*(3), 499–514.

Phinney, J. (1991). Ethnic identity and self-esteem: A review and integration. *Hispanic Journal of Behavioral Sciences*, *13*(2), 193–208.

Phinney, J., & Ong, A. (2007). Conceptualization and measurement of ethnic identity: Current status and future directions. *Journal of Counseling Psychology*, *54*(3), 271–281.

Portes, A., & Rumbaut, R. G. (2001). *Legacies: The story of the immigrant second generation*. Berkeley, CA: University of California Press.

Rideout, V. (2016). Measuring time spent with media: The Common Sense census of media use by US 8- to 18-year-olds. *Journal of Children and Media*, *10*(1), 138–144. doi: 10.1080/17482798.2016.1129808

Rosen, L. D. (2010). *Rewired: Understanding the igeneration and the way they learn*. New York, NY: Palgrave Macmillan.

Saenz, R., Hwang, S. S., Aguirre, B. E., & Anderson, R. N. (1995). Persistence and change in Asian identity among children of intermarried couples. *Sociological Perspectives*, *38*(2), 175–194.

Salomone, R. C. (2010). *True American: Language, identity, and the education of immigrant children*. Cambridge, MA: Harvard University Press.

Sears, D. O., Fu, M., Henry, P. J., & Bui, K. (2003). The origins and persistence of ethnic identity among the "new immigrant" groups. *Social Psychology*, *66*(4), 419–437.

Semyonov, M. (1997). On the cost of being an immigrant in Israel: The effects of tenure, origin and gender. *Research in Stratification and Mobility*, *15*, 115–131.

Song, A. M. (2003). *Choosing ethnic identity*. Cambridge, MA: Polity Press.

Subervi-Velez, F. (1986). The mass media and ethnic assimilation and pluralism: A review and research proposal with special focus on Hispanics. *Communication Research*, *13*, 71–96.

Subramanian, M. (2010). *Brown enough: Technology, media, and ethnic identity development in the lives of South Asian American young women* (Doctoral dissertation).

Thai, H. C. (2002). Formation of ethnic identity among second-generation Vietnamese Americans. In P. G. Min (Ed.), *The second generation: Ethnic identity among Asian Americans* (53–83). Walnut Creek, CA: AltaMira Press.

Tuan, M. (1998). Neither *real* Americans nor *real* Asians? Multigeneration Asian ethnics navigating the terrain of authenticity. *Qualitative Sociology*, *22*(2), 105–125.

Vygotsky, L. (1978). *Mind in society: The development of higher psychological processes*. Cambridge, MA: Harvard University Press.

Wakefield, W. D., & Hudley, C. (2007). Ethnic and racial identity and adolescent well-being. *Theories into Practice*, *46*(2), 147–154.

Wardyga, B. J. (2012). *The relationship between text message volume and formal writing performance among upper level high school students and college freshmen*. (Doctoral dissertation). Retrieved from http://digitalcommons.liberty.edu/cgi/viewcontent.cgi?article=1577&context=doctoral

Xie, W. (2005). Virtual space, real identity: Exploring cultural identity of Chinese diaspora in virtual community. *Telematics and Informatics*, *22*, 395–404.

Yi, Y. (2009). Adolescent literacy and identity construction among 1.5 generation students: From a transnational perspective. *Journal of Asian Pacific Communication*, *19*(1), 100–129.

Zhou, M. (2001). Straddling different worlds: The acculturation of Vietnamese refugee children. In R. Rumbaut & A. Portes (Eds.), *Ethnicities: Children of immigrants in America* (pp. 187–227). Berkeley, CA: University of California Press.

# APPENDIX A

## Interview Protocol

### Biographical Information: Who Are the Interviewees?

1. Please tell me your current age, place of birth, and number of years you have been in U.S. if you were not born here.
2. How many siblings do you have? Do you have extended family here in the U.S.? Who? Where? Do you have any family in Korea? Who? Where?
3. Which language are you more proficient at, Korean or English? What language do your parents speak? What language do you use at home? In what situations do you speak your secondary language?
4. What do you feel about your Korean fluency and English fluency? Why?
5. What are your parents' occupations?
6. To what religion, if any, do you belong? Do you practice the religion? In what ways?
7. Have you been to Korea? When? How long did you stay? Who did you see? Where did you go? What did you do there? Did you celebrate any special occasions there? What impressed you most? What did you enjoy? What did you not enjoy?

8. How would you describe your inner circle of friends? Who is in your close circle of friends? Are they your co-ethnic friends or American friends? (Racial/ethnic categories)? Does it make a difference to you? In what ways?

## Photo-Elicitation Interview Questions

1. With the photos you took, please explain what is happening in each image.
2. Please tell me why you chose to take those pictures.
3. What, if anything, is important about each picture?
4. Please tell me whether there are any photographs you wished you could have taken but did not or could not.
5. Please select your three favorite pictures – the pictures you feel best represent yourself – and explain why they are your favorite.

## Digital Media Uses/Usage Questions

1. What kinds of digital media devices do you own? (Smartphone? Video game console? Internet [laptop/desktop/tablet], MP3 player?)
2. For each digital media device you own, please tell me when, where, how long, and how you use it differently from other devices?
3. What is your daily digital media use routine? (Before and after school? During school? Afternoon? During meals? In the evening? Before going to sleep? Weekdays vs. weekends)
4. Are there any programs you watch regularly using your digital media device? Any video games you play regularly? Internet sites you visit regularly? Do you chat using mobile devices or computer regularly?
5. Do you keep up … and if so, how do you keep up with news in the U.S.? What are your sources?
6. How does your family keep up with news in the U.S.? What are their sources?
7. How do your friends keep up with news in the U.S.? What are their sources?
8. How do you keep up with news about Korea? Any sources?

9. How does your family keep up with news about Korea? Any sources?
10. How do your friends keep up with news about Korea? Any sources?
11. How would you describe your TV viewing habits? Prompts: Which programs? With whom? Why? Do you take special notice of Koreans you encounter in the media? How does it make you feel to see Koreans in the media?
12. How often do you watch movies? Which ones? Where (Theatre? DVD? Blu-ray?)? With whom do you watch movies? What types of movies do you watch? Why? Do you watch Korean dramas? Do you watch from DMB (Digital Multimedia Broadcasting)?
13. How often do you listen to K-pop? Do you have any favorite K-pop singers? Why?
14. How do you feel about using the internet? For what purposes do you use it? Do you visit certain web sites? What sites do you have bookmarked? Korean web sites? American web sites?
15. How often do you read Korean news (off/online)? Where do you get them?

## Identity: How Do They Identify Themselves and How Are They Identified by Others?

1. How often do you talk about Korean news/events with your friends? What issues come up while talking with your friends?
2. How do you feel about talking about news/events (American and/or Korean) with your family? What kind of news events do you discuss?
3. How do you identify yourself? Korean or American? Anything else?
4. In what ways do you consider yourself American? Why or why not?
5. In what ways do you consider yourself Korean? Why or why not?
6. Do you consider yourself Korean American? What does it mean to you?
7. Do you celebrate … And if so, how do you feel about celebrating *Chusok* or *Suhl-Nahl* (Korean holidays) with your family?

# APPENDIX B

## Survey Questionnaire

## Part I: Digital Media Landscape

Please choose **ALL** answer choices that apply.

1. I often use ____________________.
   (a) smartphone
   (b) tablet computer/iPad
   (c) mp3 player/iPod
   (d) desktop or laptop computer
   (e) video game console (e.g.,Wii)

Please choose the best answer.

2. How often do you use the internet on the media devices you answered in question 1?

| | Many times a day | Once or twice a day | Once every few days | About once a week | A couple times a month | About once a month or less |
|---|---|---|---|---|---|---|
| smartphone | 1 | 2 | 3 | 4 | 5 | 6 |
| tablet computer/iPad | 1 | 2 | 3 | 4 | 5 | 6 |

| | Many times a day | Once or twice a day | Once every few days | About once a week | A couple times a month | About once a month or less |
|---|---|---|---|---|---|---|
| mp3 player/iPod | 1 | 2 | 3 | 4 | 5 | 6 |
| desktop or laptop computer | 1 | 2 | 3 | 4 | 5 | 6 |
| video game console (e.g., Wii) | 1 | 2 | 3 | 4 | 5 | 6 |

3. When you surf the internet on digital media, you often go to ______.
   (a) Korean websites (b) English websites (c) Both

4. Please indicate which of the following you explored on the internet. Please **select every answer that applies.**
   (a) Korean dramas, variety/reality shows, movies, or clips
   (b) Korean pop
   (c) Korean celebrities
   (d) Korean clothing
   (e) Korean food
   (f) News and current events in Korea
   (g) Information about Korean history
   (h) Information about Korean religion
   (i) Information about Korean holidays
   (j) Information about Korean politics
   (k) Information about Korean geography

5. How often do you watch Korean dramas/movies?
   (a) never
   (b) very rarely
   (c) rarely
   (d) occasionally
   (e) very frequently

6. How often do you watch Korean TV programs, including variety/reality shows?
   (a) never
   (b) very rarely
   (c) rarely
   (d) occasionally
   (e) very frequently

7. Watching Korean TV programs helps me to improve Korean language.
   (a) strongly disagree
   (b) disagree
   (c) neutral
   (d) agree
   (e) strongly agree

8. Which communication form do you engage the most with your smartphone?

| | Many times a day | Once or twice a day | Once every few days | About once a week | A couple times a month | About once a month or less |
|---|---|---|---|---|---|---|
| Texting | 1 | 2 | 3 | 4 | 5 | 6 |
| Calling | 1 | 2 | 3 | 4 | 5 | 6 |

9. When you engage in texting, do you sometimes use language(s) other than English?
   (a) Yes (b) No
   If you answered **YES**, what language(s) do you use? ______________

10. Which text messaging application do you use most often in your social daily social interactions? Please select **ALL** the choices that apply.

| | Many times a day | Once or twice a day | Once every few days | About once a week | A couple times a month | About once a month or less |
|---|---|---|---|---|---|---|
| KakaoTalk | 1 | 2 | 3 | 4 | 5 | 6 |
| Facebook | 1 | 2 | 3 | 4 | 5 | 6 |
| Skype | 1 | 2 | 3 | 4 | 5 | 6 |

11. What kinds of social media do you use for your social media practices? Please select **ALL** the choices that apply.
    (a) Facebook
    (b) Instagram
    (c) Twitter
    (d) YouTube
    (e) Pinterest
    (f) MySpace

(g) Tumblr
(h) Reddit
(i) Others (write in): ____________________

## Part II: Ethnic Identity Questions (MEIM-R)

Please indicate the extent to which you agree with the following statements:

| | Strongly disagree | Disagree | Neutral | Agree | Strongly agree |
|---|---|---|---|---|---|
| 12. I have spent time trying to find out more about my own ethnic group, such as its history, traditions, customs, and pop cultures. | 1 | 2 | 3 | 4 | 5 |
| 13. I have a strong sense of belonging to my own ethnic group. | 1 | 2 | 3 | 4 | 5 |
| 14. I understand pretty well what my ethnic group membership means to me. | 1 | 2 | 3 | 4 | 5 |
| 15. I have often done things that will help me understand my ethnic background better. | 1 | 2 | 3 | 4 | 5 |
| 16. I have often talked to other people in order to learn more about my ethnic group. | 1 | 2 | 3 | 4 | 5 |
| 17. I feel a strong attachment towards my own ethnic group. | 1 | 2 | 3 | 4 | 5 |

In this country, people come from a lot of different cultures and there are many different words to describe the different backgrounds or ethnic groups that people come from. Some examples of the names of ethnic groups are Mexican American, Hispanic, Black, Asian American, American Indian,

Anglo American, and White. Every person is born into an ethnic group, or sometimes two groups, but people differ on how important their ethnicity is to them, how they feel about it, and how much their behavior is affected by it. These questions are about your ethnicity or your ethnic group and how you feel about it or react to it. Please **fill in the blank**:

In terms of ethnic group, I consider myself to be ______________________.

## Part III: Demographics

18. What is your age now? ( ) years old.
19. What is your gender?
    (a) Male ( ) (b) Female ( )
20. Where were you born?
    (a) Korea (b) U.S. (c) Other: ______________________
21. Age of immigration (if you were born outside of the U.S.): __________

# INDEX

## A



## B

# C



# D



# E

## F



## G



## H



## I



## J



## K

## L



## M



## N



## O



## P

## R



## S



## T



## U



## Y

# mediated youth

Sharon R. Mazzarella
*General Editor*

Grounded in cultural studies, books in this series will study the cultures, artifacts, and media of children, tweens, teens, and college-aged youth. Whether studying television, popular music, fashion, sports, toys, the Internet, self-publishing, leisure, clubs, school, cultures/activities, film, dance, language, tie-in merchandising, concerts, subcultures, or other forms of popular culture, books in this series go beyond the dominant paradigm of traditional scholarship on the effects of media/culture on youth. Instead, authors endeavor to understand the complex relationship between youth and popular culture. Relevant studies would include, but are not limited to studies of how youth negotiate their way through the maze of corporately-produced mass culture; how they themselves have become cultural producers; how youth create "safe spaces" for themselves within the broader culture; the political economy of youth culture industries; the representational politics inherent in mediated coverage and portrayals of youth; and so on. Books that provide a forum for the "voices" of the young are particularly encouraged. The source of such voices can range from in-depth interviews and other ethnographic studies to textual analyses of cultural artifacts created by youth.

For further information about the series and submitting manuscripts, please contact:

SHARON R. MAZZARELLA
School of Communication Studies
James Madison University
Harrisonburg, VA 22807

To order other books in this series, please contact our Customer Service Department at:

(800) 770-LANG (within the U.S.)
(212) 647-7706 (outside the U.S.)
(212) 647-7707 FAX

Or browse online by series at WWW.PETERLANG.COM

www.ingramcontent.com/pod-product-compliance
Ingram Content Group UK Ltd.
Pitfield, Milton Keynes, MK11 3LW, UK
UKHW021835100926
8556IPUK00004B/354

9 781433 157288